The nature of proof

THE BOBBS-MERRILL SERIES IN *Speech Communication*

RUSSEL R. WINDES, *Editor*

Queens College of the City University of New York

ERWIN P. BETTINGHAUS

Michigan State University

The nature

of proof

SECOND EDITION

The Bobbs-Merrill Company, Inc.

INDIANAPOLIS AND NEW YORK

Editor's foreword

Perhaps the most difficult problem faced by the communicator in any speech communication situation is that of organizing and processing his ideas and supporting materials in order that his **message** to his audience be **believable.** Too often the communicator moves through message preparation unable to arrange his material cogently, unable to test the probity of that material, and unable to predict what his audience's reaction to his message will be once the message is presented. In short, the communicator normally defends a proposition; he builds a case for his proposition through arguments he asks his audience to believe, but his persuasiveness (the degree to which his message is found acceptable) hinges on the modes of proof he elects to use and how these proofs are structured. Consequently, the study of **proof** is vital to the student of communication.

Most of us use the word "proof" fairly loosely. While this is not a capital crime, it is a lesser offense which tends to blur our perception of what is happening when people communicate with each other. For proof is not, after all, an object, or an assertion as to fact written on a note card, nor even a formulary statement describing relationships. Rather, as Professor Bettinghaus points out in **The Nature of Proof,** "Proof is the process of using evidence to secure belief in an idea or statement." Proof, then, is not something that one drudgingly collects at a library or fabricates at the cafeteria. It is a vital **process** which is central to all ongoing communicative activities.

All of us need, almost constantly, to influence the beliefs of others, if for no other reason than to control the decisions which affect our lives. To influence beliefs we must be more or less adept in the process of marshalling information for the purpose of presenting a picture of the world to others which will cause them to react favorably to our ideas and conclusions. **The Nature of Proof,** then, is a treatise in the ways an individual engaged in speech communication may responsibly influence beliefs through evidence and inference.

To understand the proof process, the reader must comprehend the nature of belief and the place of belief in the communication of ideas. He must also grasp the nature of evidence, of inference, and of judgments which motivate people to the acceptance of an idea or proposition. And, importantly, he must understand the ways in which ideas can be presented to an audience, and he must develop a certain predictability skill relating to how various audiences may react in various ways to differing kinds of proof. Professor Bettinghaus addresses himself to these problems in an attempt to acquaint the reader with the processes and methods of securing belief.

The study of proof is implicitly present in the study of every subject. Any teacher, no matter what subject he teaches, must constantly ask his students, "Why do you believe that?" Consequently, a book on the nature of proof has a potentially universal relevance. The first edition of Professor Bettinghaus's book (1966), for instance, has been used in departments of history, anthropology, sociology, and English, as well as in departments of speech and communication and in interdisciplinary programs such as "pre-law." The book has become most popular, of course, in the introductory course in speech communication, in advanced courses in argument and persuasion, in small-group communication courses, and in some graduate courses dealing with the philosophy of research and the testing of hypotheses.

What was so very exciting about Professor Bettinghaus's first edition was its use of material from the social sciences to describe the proof process. Studies of proof have traditionally been organized around two questions: What proofs are necessary to establish a belief? What kinds of proofs (and beliefs) are necessary to influence a given auditor or audience? Prior to the appearance of **The Nature of**

Proof writers in speech communication attempted to answer the questions primarily through an artistic approach to the study of communication. Professor Bettinghaus did not ignore the artistic approach, but he added to it findings from the science of communication—the systematic and controlled investigation of human interaction.

This second edition of **The Nature of Proof** retains the basic format and approach of the first edition, but new material based on research findings since 1966 has been added. Material has been updated in terms of examples, and significant changes have been made in the organization of the material to facilitate teaching and learning. These changes have made the book even more lucid and have clarified a number of issues which earlier were still under investigation.

Russel R. Windes

Contents

The nature of proof

ONE

The nature of proof

Introduction

What do **you** believe in? Do you believe that it is bad luck for a black cat to cross your path? Do you believe that if you step on a crack, you'll break your mother's back? What leads you to believe that the world is round, that man has evolved from lower animal forms, or that the Detroit Lions are the best team in professional football? Each of these questions is concerned with the presence or absence of a **belief** and with the links between events that cause us to hold a certain belief.

Throughout much of recorded history, man has attempted to link one set of events with another and to show that because one event happened, we should believe or disbelieve in some position. Science, history, jurisprudence, and religion are all concerned with the relationships that are to be obtained between sets of events and the conclusions we draw from a consideration of those events. Whenever someone has become convinced that he **can** establish the cause of an event, he says that he has **proved** it. This book is about **proof** and the role it plays in the establishment of beliefs and the preparation of messages about those beliefs.

3

Modes of proof have changed greatly over the centuries, but the concept of proof is recognizable over a span of two thousand years. Ancient Greeks recognized confessions obtained from the torture of witnesses as valid evidence—and perfectly good proof—in their courts. During the Roman era, a defendant was allowed to parade his weeping wife and children before the judge as proof of his innocence. During the Middle Ages, the "water test" could establish the proof of a man's guilt. The accused was thrown into a lake or pond. If he swam, he was judged guilty; if he drowned, he was believed to have been innocent. During the American colonial period, in the late 1600s, colonists accepted as proof in some courts the testimony that individuals were witches because milk turned sour after they had visited the cow barn.

Americans no longer accept the water test as evidence of innocence or guilt, and most of us do not believe in witches. Nevertheless, we do remain interested in proof. We use the word in several ways, and we vary greatly in our ideas of what to accept as proof, but we realize that one of the communicator's main tasks is to supply enough evidence so that his audience will say, "That is enough. You have proved your case."

The nuclear physicist, the psychologist, the lawyer, and the policeman are all interested in proof, as are the speaker at a PTA meeting, the newspaper reporter, the college debater, the housewife buying soap flakes, and the man listening to a political speech. The needs of speakers and listeners will differ, but establishing belief through proof is important for many communication situations. The scope of this book may be illustrated from the following series of situations which hinge on an understanding of the concept of proof.

1. **Perry Mason** and other television shows have made most Americans familiar with the courtroom scene in which the prosecuting attorney is attempting to convict a defendant of armed robbery. The task of the prosecution in such a situation is to show clearly that the defendant did commit the robbery. After presenting the evidence and witnesses to the crime, the prosecutor may conclude by saying, "The evidence shows clearly that the defendant did commit the robbery for which he has been charged and should be adjudged as 'Guilty' by the members of the jury."

2. The other side of the same courtroom situation is represented by the defense attorney. The defense must demonstrate that the prose-

cution has not proved its case against the defendant. Witnesses and evidence for the defense will try to establish that the defendant could not have been in a position to commit the alleged crime. The defense attorney may conclude by telling the jury that "the prosecution has failed to prove that my client did commit this crime."

3. If one loses a sum of money or a pocketbook and goes to a police station or the lost-and-found section of a store, he will be asked to "prove" that the money is his. He will be asked to show in some fashion that what was found was in fact what he lost, as well as to establish his right to the money or lost valuables.

4. Imagine a situation in which a number of small boys are playing. One of them declares, "I'm the toughest guy in the whole bunch!" It is unlikely that he will be allowed to get away without being asked to "prove it!" A similar situation may be seen in the familiar barroom scene when the tough, two-fisted drinker shouts, "I can lick any man in the house!" Again, he will be asked to "prove it!"

5. Every four years the United States elects a new President or retains an incumbent President. Each of the candidates presents a platform consisting of statements of what he intends to do if elected. The political campaign consists of attempts by each man to prove that he should be elected. He does so by showing that he has the better platform or that his qualifications will enable him to carry out his ideas more successfully than the other man. Once more, proof is important, but it seems to be a different kind of proof from that called for from the small boy or the loser of a twenty-dollar bill.

6. Consider the scientist. His whole professional life is involved with proof. He may come to believe that cancer is caused by a virus. His belief, however, is not enough. He must be able to **prove** to his colleagues and the rest of the world that his hypotheses are correct.

7. Finally, one may look at recent campaigns supporting the fluoridation of water supplies. The proponents of fluoridation claim that taking this step will reduce the number of cavities children are likely to have. The opponents of fluoridation say there is no **proof** this will happen, and they further point to possible damages to health that they feel are linked to fluoridation. Regardless of which side wins the referendum, the newspapers are likely to say after the vote is in that one side or the other "proved its case."

Each of these situations is different, but each uses the term **proof.** Each situation seems to involve the **testing of ideas.** Originally, to "prove" something meant to ". . . make trial of, or to test the genuineness or qualities of . . ." a thing.[1] For the speaker, proof is still linked to testing, and although the ways in which we test ideas differ, the basic process is still the same.

Although the seven situations described above seem different in many respects, some elements in each of the situations are common to the seven and common to all communication situations where proof is involved. Let us look at them again and ask just **how** the individuals involved attempt to test their ideas—to prove their case.

1. The prosecuting attorney must be able to show that the defendant did indeed commit the crime, and he must be able to establish his case to the satisfaction of the jury. The prosecutor must find witnesses who will swear they saw the defendant commit the crime, or he must produce evidence establishing the presence of the defendant at the scene of the crime and evidence establishing that the defendant had a motive to commit the crime. Regardless of the specific nature of the evidence produced by the prosecutor, he will be limited in his effort to show that the defendant is guilty to **making statements,** producing witnesses who make statements, or **producing exhibits.** He will win his case only if the jury **believes** the witnesses he produces or is swayed by the statements he makes.

2. The defense attorney does not have (under our system of jurisprudence) as difficult a task as does the prosecutor. He must merely establish some doubt that the defendant could have committed the crime. His method, however, is much the same as that of the prosecutor. He is limited to trying to show through a series of **statements** or **exhibits** that his client is innocent. He may produce a witness who will swear that he saw the defendant in another town on the night of the robbery. Or he may bring in a picture that purports to show the defendant playing cards in a hotel on the other side of town at the time of the robbery. He can only win his case if the jury **believes** the witnesses he produces, the exhibits he displays, or the statements he makes.

3. The loser of some money might give the serial numbers of the bills he lost as evidence that the money belongs to him and not to someone else, or he might describe in detail exactly where he lost the money. The police, however, will not return the money until enough

[1] **The Oxford Universal Dictionary on Historical Principles,** 3d ed. (Oxford: Clarendon Press, 1955), p. 1607.

evidence is produced to make them believe that the claimant is indeed the owner of the money.

4. The small boy who wants to prove he is the toughest boy on the block or the barfly who wants to prove he can lick any man in the house has several alternatives. He may make a series of statements suggesting that he is the biggest or the roughest or can jump higher than any other person in the group. The boy or the barfly may offer to let others feel his muscles, or he may offer to fight. In either case, the challenger makes statements or demonstrates his abilities until the others decide to believe him.

5. The Presidential candidate cannot ask the electorate to feel his muscles—at least not literally. The candidate is confined to words. He must make statements about his past actions, his present intentions, and his future expectations in the hope that the voters will eventually come to believe the statements he makes and cast their votes for him.

6. The scientist must also depend on the beliefs of other people testing his ideas and hypotheses. He may make a series of statements in order to show that his hypotheses are correct, or he may offer a series of demonstrations. For example, he may show his listeners a series of fossils and then claim that these exhibit a particular relationship to present-day animals. The great anthropologist L. S. B. Leakey produced a number of fossil remains from Africa that he claimed were very distant relations of present-day mankind. The average viewer looking at Professor Leakey's exhibits might easily conclude that all they look like is a bunch of rocks. Unable to interpret the exhibits himself, he might yet decide to believe in Leakey's hypotheses because he has developed some belief in Professor Leakey himself.

7. The case of the fluoridation campaign is perhaps most representative of the role that proof plays in message preparation. Both sides appeal to the electorate to accept the position that they represent. They use statements made in speeches, newspapers, and advertisements. Both sides are limited in their efforts by the amount of material available and the time they have. They must prepare their communications in such a way that listeners will want to accept their statements as proof of their position. They can present statistics showing that fluoridation results in 35 percent fewer cavities after ten years of use. They can show pictures of teeth which have turned black from the application of too much fluoride. They can appeal to religious

beliefs against adding medicines to water supplies. They can appeal to economic beliefs and point to the savings on dentist bills. Whatever is presented is done so in order to secure **belief** in a statement by the electorate. The proponents want the voters to believe the statement, "Fluoridation should be adopted," while the opponents of fluoridation want belief in the statement, "Fluoridation should not be adopted."

One common element in each of our examples is the **concept of belief.** When listeners or readers believe, the communicator has proved his case. This is the goal of all persuasion and the reason for attempting such a difficult thing as proof. Belief is of such importance that Chapter 2 will be devoted entirely to a discussion of belief and oral communication.

A second common element is the means by which proof may be obtained. The communicator who wishes to prove his case, and thus secure belief in his ideas, may do so only by producing **evidence** to support his ideas. That is, he must make statements or produce exhibits or provide demonstrations that support his case. He must have evidence, and it must be related in some way to the proposition in which he wishes to secure the belief of his receivers. The nature and types of evidence are discussed fully in Chapter 4.

The common elements in these seven situations suggest a definition of proof: **Proof is the process of using evidence to secure belief in an idea or statement.**

This definition forms the basis for the remainder of this book. The definition will be expanded with two goals in mind: (1) the reader should learn to use evidence to secure belief in his ideas, and (2) the reader should learn to listen to evidence being presented by another in such a way as to be able to test the adequacy of that material as support for the other's idea.

Speech communication and communicator intent

The nuclear physicist, the psychologist, and the policeman are concerned with proof in situations that do not necessarily involve oral communication. The discussion in this volume, however, will be limited to situations involving speech communication. This limitation is not at all an inhibiting one. Most of our ideas, memories, beliefs, and knowledge have been gained through communication, and the greatest part of our communication activity is through speech communication, through talking and listening to others.

Many students of speech communication argue that all communication has a persuasive nature. The author tends to agree with this stand and to subscribe to the type of speech analysis that stresses the necessity for attitude change even when the stated intent of the communicator is only to have an individual learn a series of facts. In the light of this point of view, it will be useful to look specifically at the relationships which exist between "proof" and "belief" on the one hand, and "inform" and "persuade" on the other.

Speakers have **goals** in mind when they engage in communication. We do not ordinarily begin talking to someone else unless we have some idea of what we wish the individual to do as a result of our conversation. If we were to ask a speaker what he wanted as the result of a particular speech, he might say, "I just wanted to give the receiver some information which he did not have." In such a situation, we would say that the speaker's goal was **to inform.** In another situation, the speaker might say, "I know that he doesn't believe in fluoridation, and I wanted to change his attitude toward fluoridation." In this case, we would say that the speaker's goal was **to persuade.** Regardless of whether the speaker has informing or persuading as his goal, he will need to provide **proof in order to secure belief** in the statements he makes. Thus proof and belief become the processes that are used in both informing and persuading.

It is important to note that regardless of the stated goal of the speaker, it is rare to find a speech which is purely informative or purely persuasive in nature. At first glance, it may seem that informative speaking consists merely of a recital of statements of fact, of pieces of evidence. Indeed, many speakers may state, "I'll just give them the facts—the plain, simple facts." This is, of course, an oversimplification. The speaker may well have to persuade the listener that he is worth listening to before he can present informative statements. Furthermore, people do not necessarily learn "plain, simple facts." One may need to present evidence in the form of simple statements in order to obtain the learning of more complex facts. That is, one must **prove** by the use of simple pieces of evidence that a more complex statement is to be learned. Imagine that you wanted to teach a savage that the world is round. Your goal would clearly be to inform. In order to be sure that the savage had "learned," you would have to present many small pieces of evidence. Only in this way could you be sure that the savage finally understood your position. Only then could you assume that your listener had actually learned the materials of interest. This same kind of analysis of the learning process and its relation to proof is also necessary for the kind of learning situation in which one wishes the receiver to be able to perform some task at the conclusion of the speech. If the objective is to teach him to thread a moving-picture projector, it must be accomplished through the presentation of small bits of material, taking him step-by-step through the process. The presentation of material in informative communication is not merely the presentation of simple facts. Proof is needed in order to make the listener feel there is some reason for learning in the first place; it is also needed in order to secure the learning of complex materials.

Persuasive communication, while aimed toward a goal of changing attitudes or inducing some change in behavior, is normally not purely persuasive in nature. It may be possible to produce a speech in which it is not necessary to present some information before being able to secure a change in attitude or behavior. But it is extremely difficult to do so. Even the most emotional, biased speaker will have some statements of fact, some evidence that must be learned in his speech.

An example of the importance of evidence in changing attitudes can be observed in considering the alternatives open to a speaker supporting a school bond campaign. He could operate completely in the area of opinions and say, "We need more money for schools. This is a good proposal. Our children deserve the best, and this bond campaign will give it to them." Here, the communicator does not require an individual to learn anything. The listener need merely believe in the speaker's final proposition. It might be more persuasive for him to say,

> Last week our schools were visited by the State Department of Education. Officials from that department report that we will lose our state accreditation if we do not provide more classrooms and more teachers for our basic courses. If we lose our state accreditation, our children cannot be accepted at the state university. In order for them to have the same advantages as the children of other school systems, it is necessary for us to pass the proposed bond issue.

The message is persuasive, but the speaker finds it necessary for the receiver to become informed about some of the past events which led him to make his current proposal.

Our examples should have served to reinforce the point that whether the overall goal of the speech is to inform or to persuade, most messages have both informative and persuasive elements within them. To attain either goal, a communicator must present evidence in order to secure belief in the propositions he is advancing. Proof is just as important when the intention of the communicator is to persuade as it is when he is attempting to get a receiver to learn a series of statements of fact.

There is one special situation which deserves mention. In a formal debate, two or more communicators representing different points of view attempt to sway an audience to their different ways of thinking. A debate, in real life, represents a situation in which two individuals are for opposite sides of some policy, e.g., for or against aid to parochial schools, or when two aspirants for public office debate the merits of their respective platforms. Evidence plays a doubly important role in this situation. Possibly, when only one speaker is advocating a particular position, a listener might agree with his proposition after the presentation of a minimum amount of evidence. But when several speakers are present and different points of view are represented, he will not agree so easily. The nature of the evidence presented by different speakers is an important factor in determining the winner of the debate. There are, of course, many other important factors. The speaker with the better delivery will have an advantage; so will the speaker with the best-known reputation, the speaker with the best choice of words, and the speaker who has marshalled the most acceptable set of evidence for his position or who can support his position with the clearest reasoning.

In some situations, delivery is undoubtedly the determining factor in an individual's decision to accept the conclusions presented by one side in a debate. In others, the reputation of the speaker or his choice of words may be decisive. In many others, the decision may be made on the basis of the evidence presented. Whether the debate is in a courtroom, where materials are presented according to an elaborate set of rules, or in a Parent-Teachers meeting debating the merits of compulsory gymnastics for high-school students, the communicator who brings a better set of evidence to bear on his topic has an advantage.

Most of us tend to look at evidence as useful only in a courtroom. Television drama and newspaper coverage certainly support that tendency. But evidence is important in all speaking situations. Whether one is sitting across the table from a friend, or with a group of friends, or speaking from a public platform, he needs evidence to secure the attention of his auditors, to interest them in learning the material he presents, and to get them to accept his proposals.

Certainly, one cannot argue that the mere presentation of various kinds of evidence will necessarily result in more effective communication. But unless a speaker knows how to use evidence appropriately, his possession of other communication skills will not make for effective communication.

Material evidence and our language system

Up to now in our discussion, there has been an implicit assumption that evidence is concerned only with facts, that only statements of fact may be used as evidence. Such a view is too narrow.

The sentence intended to inform the listener about some object or event in the physical world is called a **statement of fact.** Statements of fact form the basis for all evidence, whether the statement of fact is given directly as evidence or has been used to arrive at some other statement. Examples of statements of fact that might be used as evidence by a communicator include: "There are eleven fish in that tank," "There are three fingerprints on the rifle," "The paper reports that there were thirty people killed in automobile accidents last year," "The man earned $10,000 last year." These statements have a characteristic that distinguishes them from all other kinds of sentences. They can be **verified.** Statements of fact are sentences that can be labeled as either true or false. If one counted the number of fish in the tank and found there were not eleven fish but fourteen, he would label as false the statement, "There are eleven fish in that tank." Note that we do not say this statement is **not** a statement of fact. It is. But it is a false statement of fact. **Verification is a word describing the process we go through to determine whether or not a sentence is a true statement of fact or a false statement of fact.**

All statements of fact are capable of being verified. However, statements of fact can be divided into two categories, depending on the way in which we attempt verification of them. A **report** or **observation** is a statement of fact, made about physical reality, that is immediately verifiable through sense observation. An **inference** is also a statement of fact made about physical reality but it is not directly verifiable.

A report is verified by going from the statement to the real world and making an actual check. If someone tells us there are three traffic lights at a particular intersection, we can go to the intersection and count them. If we find three lights, we say that the individual made an accurate report. If we read that 9000 high-school seniors have applied for college scholarships at a particular university, we may go to the registrar at that university, ask him for the file of scholarship applications, and proceed to count them. The results of our counting will determine whether the statement was accurate or not.

If one actually had to verify personally all the reports to which he is exposed every day, most of his time would be spent in the process of verification. Moreover, many observational statements are either difficult or impossible to verify. The average individual could not verify the statement, "The tallest tree in the world is 372 feet high." The statement is a report. It could only be verified by measuring all the trees in the world and finding that none was taller than 372 feet. But most of us rely on verification attested to by other individuals. Everyone relies on verifications produced by others to a surprising extent. Almost all statements of fact that one reads in the daily newspaper, for instance, are believed or disbelieved without the personal verification of the reader. One reads textbooks on history, science, art, and chemistry and seldom bothers to check the accuracy of their observations.

When an individual takes a report made by someone else as true and does not verify the statements in the report himself, he places trust in the reputation of the other communicator not to make statements that are false. In such a situation, if one cannot personally verify the statement, he employs a second method of verification: he checks the reputation of the communicator making the statement of fact. Chapter 4 will look at methods of checking statements that cannot be personally verified.

In many of the most interesting communication situations, statements of fact are not used directly. Rather, reports and observation statements are used to make another type of statement of fact that we call an **inference.** Inferences are based on observations, on physi-

cal reality, but they cannot be verified directly. Some examples of
inferences are: "The man was afraid," "Red China wants to start a
Third World War," "The girl doesn't like the boy," "Our children are
getting an inferior education," "The governor doesn't want to give the
university enough money." All these statements are inferential. Their
truth or falsity depends on some consideration of an observation or a
set of observations, but they cannot be directly verified through
sensory channels.

Consider the statement, "The man was afraid." This statement
might be made on the basis of observing that the man was sweating
or had turned pale or had run away. After making the observations,
the observer makes the inference. Note that the inference may be
incorrect. It could well be that the man was sick, and that the sickness
caused him to sweat and turn pale. Now take the statement, "The
man had a poor attitude toward his job." This inference may have
been generated from observations that the man was late to work, that
he took overlong coffee breaks, that he left early, or that his work was
not so good as that done by others. The statement "The man had a
poor attitude toward his job" was made on the basis of a series of
observations or reports, but it is not an observation. It is an inference,
and like all inferences, it is susceptible to being incorrect. It might be
equally true that the man had not received proper training on the job.

Inferential statements are important in any consideration of the
concept of proof. In many sciences and arts, inferences form the
basic materials with which one works. Any inferential statement is a
statement made about a portion of physical reality that cannot be
known directly. Thus one must make inferences when he wants to
find out what Indian tribes inhabited the United States one thousand
years ago. He also needs inferences when he wants to find out who
committed a particular crime, when he attempts to make medical
diagnoses, or when he wishes to make statements about the intentions of the Soviet Union toward the United States.

In the detailed examination of kinds of evidence in the second part
of this book, inferential statements are shown to serve as a basic form
of evidence. But this beginning analysis should serve to alert the
reader to the two major dangers of the inferential statement. The first
has already been mentioned, i.e., the inference may be incorrectly
drawn from the observations on which it is based. The second danger
is that one may fail to recognize an inference when it is made and may

operate as if the statement were an observation rather than being based on observations. Again, a set of rules will be suggested to help in distinguishing inferential statements from statements that are reports or observations.

We have seen that statements of fact form the basis for much communication activity. There is, however, a second type of sentence that plays an important role in communication. This is the **judgmental statement.** Judgmental statements do not have a primary relationship to the physical world. Judgments include such sentences as: "San Francisco is a beautiful city," "That football team is the best in the state," "That legislator is prejudiced against my company." These statements are all judgments. They do not say much about the physical world, and they cannot be verified through sense data. They do say something about the individual making the judgment. Judgmental statements provide an indication of the kind of attitudes or values the maker of the statement holds. They no not tell one anything about the nature of the physical world, **unless** one knows something about the man making the statement. Only when something is known about the bases for a particular judgmental statement can it be used as evidence.

One means of distinguishing the judgmental from the inferential or observational statement is to look at the kinds of words in the sentence. Words such as "beautiful," "artistic," "wonderful," "horrible," "best," "good," "efficient," or "happy" are the kind of words that one typically finds in judgmental statements. They are words whose meaning will differ according to the communicator. It is certainly true that even words we think we know the meaning of may give us trouble, but words that clearly express approval or disapproval of what we are talking about identify the statement as a judgment.

Judgmental statements are tempting. They allow one to place values easily on ideas, objects, and people. When engaged in persuasion, we are strongly tempted to make a judgment serve instead of a series of factual statements, either reports or inferences. Judgments are sometimes used as material evidence, but their use is limited.

Summary

This chapter has defined proof as the process of using evidence to secure belief in an idea or statement. It has suggested that the communicator may be engaged in communication in order to inform or to persuade his listeners, or he may be engaged in that special persuasive situation we call debate. In each of these situations, the communicator is concerned with proof and with the materials of proof we call evidence. Finally, the chapter has examined the kinds of sentences which the communicator is concerned with when he selects materials to use in proving his case. Statements of fact may be divided into reports, observations, and inferential statements. Statements of fact always say something about the physical world, while a second type of statement, the judgment, says more about the individual making the statement than it does about the world. Both types of statements must be kept in mind when looking in detail at the concept of proof.

The nature of belief

The need to study belief and belief systems

In the first chapter, proof was defined as the process of using evidence to secure belief in ideas. Later chapters will be devoted to an examination of various types of evidence and the ways in which evidence can be used in constructing speech materials. Before making that examination, however, it will be helpful to look at the concept of **belief,** a goal in all communication.

Closely related to the concept of belief is the concept of **attitude.** We distinguish between them in the same manner as does Rokeach, i.e., a **belief** is any simple proposition that an individual can attest to, while an **attitude** is an enduring organization of beliefs around a situation which predisposes an individual to respond in some particular manner.[1] Thus, attitudes and beliefs can be treated in much the same way, since beliefs are the basic building blocks of attitudes. This close interrelationship will be apparent in our further treatment of the concept of belief.

The first volume in this series, **Speech Communication: A**

[1] Milton Rokeach, **Beliefs, Attitudes and Values** (San Francisco: Jossey-Bass, Inc., 1968), pp. 112–113.

Behavioral Approach by Gerald Miller, noted that all speech communication results in persuasion, in changes in the beliefs and, subsequently, changes in the attitudes of auditors. The fact that a speaker
intends only to entertain or to provide information for his audience
may obscure the fact that changes in belief or attitudes will occur
along with the intended learning or entertainment. To understand
persuasion means to understand belief, and when we say that persuasion has taken place, we are really also saying that we have
modified or changed an individual's system of beliefs in some way.

An auditor's beliefs help determine what he listens to and to whom
he is willing to listen. An auditor already favorable toward a position
we advocate is far more willing to listen to us and to believe what we
say than he would be to someone holding an opposite position. Conversely, an auditor who is disposed to a position different from our
own is less willing to listen to what we say, and changing his attitudes
and beliefs is a more difficult task. An entertainer can engage the
attention of an audience only if his auditors believe in his potential as
a humorist enough to be willing to hear him out. Thus, in a very real
sense, belief lies at the base of all attempts at communication. The
speech communicator must understand the bases for belief.

This understanding is important for two reasons. First, the speaker
must understand the concept of belief in order to phrase his message.
That is, he must know what beliefs he is interested in changing or
establishing in his listeners. Whether his stated, overt intent is persuasion or learning, the speaker must be concerned with an examination of beliefs in order to achieve his goal. When the goal is learning,
i.e., when the speaker is interested in getting a receiver to retain his
material or in developing a receiver's competency at handling difficult
material, the extent of the receiver's belief in that material may determine his willingness to expose himself to it. If a student does not
feel that mathematics will ever be of any use to him, it is not likely
that he will be interested in listening to a lecture on mathematics;
and if forced to listen, he may learn little. When the aim of the speaker
is to effect some act of overt behavior on the part of the audience, e.g.,
to obtain a vote for a candidate, he will at least have to secure the
belief of the audience in that candidate and what the candidate
stands for before the behavioral act will occur.

The second reason for the importance of an understanding of belief
is not so easy to see: the communicator must be able to **use belief to**

secure belief. He may want the listener to become favorably disposed toward a particular piece of legislation. If he knows that the listener already favors a consequence of that legislation, he may use the belief in the consequence to secure belief in the legislation. For example, many people are worried about the world population problem. They believe that the population must soon level off or the world will have serious problems in sustaining present living standards. The speaker who wishes to elicit support for a measure allowing the United States to give assistance to foreign governments in developing birth-control practices might well use his listeners' concern about the rising population to support his contentions about birth control. An advertising manager may have to secure belief in the effectiveness of a particular make of automobile. If he knows that the listener believes that engine performance is the most important attribute of any car, he might well word an advertisement something like this:

> An automobile ought to run well. In city driving, or on the open road, any car must perform consistently. That is why our company starts designing its cars from the inside out. The best automotive engineers in the country have worked to make the engine in this car perform perfectly under all driving conditions.

What the advertiser has done here is to make use of an already held belief to influence belief in a related proposition. He has used belief in one proposition to secure belief in another.

A better understanding of these two reasons for the importance of belief can be obtained by examining some communication situations where belief plays an important part in determining the speaker's success.

1. Recent years have seen the emergence of Africa as an area of major world concern. The United States has sent Peace Corps representatives there to assist the emerging African states in developing their education, health, and economic systems. The main tool the Peace Corps representative has is his ability to talk a villager into trying a new idea. Many representatives of the Peace Corps have, however, run into serious difficulties in their attempts at persuasion. The belief systems of many Africans are quite different from those of a Peace corpsman. In spite of intense efforts by Christian missionaries and a thousand years of Moslem proselyting, basic African belief patterns in magic, witchcraft, and ritual still prevail in many rural areas.

For instance, a sick tribesman might not believe that disease is caused by germs or viruses. He is more likely to believe that his illness is caused by magic or witchcraft and will blame his misfortunes on the machinations of a witch doctor presumably hired by his enemies. The corpsman might believe that his job will be easy. He draws a sample of blood (from his own arm, because the native will not let his blood be drawn for fear that it will be used against him by a witch doctor) and shows the native that there are "little animals" in the blood. He then explains that similar "little animals" in the tribesman's blood are causing him to feel bad. Simple? Probably not. Basic belief patterns are not so easily changed. The native's reply might be, "What witch doctor placed the little animals in your blood?" If he feels friendly toward the poor misguided Peace corpsman, he might even offer to tell him what witch doctor to hire to get the little animals out of his blood.

2. Every year, shortly after the Thanksgiving holiday has passed, small children all over the United States begin to talk about Santa Claus. Their belief in the toy-giving potential of the little fat man with the reindeer and sleigh has amazed and delighted generations of parents. During this annual period, compliance with parental requests is at an all-time high, a large portion of it seemingly the result of a belief in Santa Claus. But shortly after Christmas, appeals to Santa Claus have little or no effect on the behavior of the same small children. When the child reaches school age, moreover, he usually becomes quite suspicious about the good saint's existence. This belief is certainly related to behavior, but it is quite different from the African's belief in witchcraft. If a belief is not a dominant and persistent part of an individual's personality, it cannot be successfully used in preparing messages or securing behavior for very long. Because the belief in Santa Claus tends to disappear at an early age, it may be used to effect behavior only for a short time.

3. In several areas of the United States, small religious sects believe in extremely literal interpretations of the Bible. Their interpretations extend to their analyses of the physical world around them, and they explain physical phenomena solely in terms of words used in the Bible. Several years ago, newspapers in the United States printed a story about the minister in a small Southern town who told his congregation that the sky was located forty miles above the earth and that it consisted of a covering separating Heaven from Earth. For this minister,

the stars were holes in the covering, and he firmly maintained that when we were finally able to reach the sky, we would find Heaven on the other side of the covering. When reporters talked to him about evidence obtained from modern science, he refused to listen, saying only, "You will see that I am right when we are able to fly that high." One wonders what has happened to his beliefs since Neil Armstrong and Buzz Aldrin stepped onto the surface of the moon. The basic beliefs of the minister helped determine what he listened to and what he accepted as proof. It will require very strong evidence to change beliefs and attitudes in this situation.

4. The past few years have seen a great awakening of interest in the quality of our environment. Air and water pollution are becoming subjects of attention and speculation for many Americans. To read the newspapers and magazines, one might get the impression that we are all in agreement with the proposition that our air must be cleaned up, that our streams must be allowed to run waste-free, and that we must provide recreational facilities for all our citizens. One might think that it would be easy to secure acceptance of programs to improve the quality of our environment. However, the problem is not so easily solved. Most of us also hold beliefs affirming the importance of industry to our country, affirming the rights of people to hold property and to do with that property as they see fit, and affirming the rights of government to build roads and bridges. What happens when a proposal to clean up a particular stream runs up against opposition from an industry which must put chemical wastes in the water in order to continue its operation? What happens when a marsh is filled in to make room for a road to carry people to their work in a significantly shorter time? What happens when we propose to clean up air pollution by eliminating the automobile from our streets? What happens when a property owner on a lake shore has his property taken by the government to make a park? In these situations, beliefs come into conflict. It will be difficult to show individuals that they have to give up one set of beliefs if they are to continue to believe in another set.

In these four sample situations, the beliefs involved differ in content and in kind. The differences in the situations are also important in determining the ways in which communication will be initiated and received. Other variables further point up the importance of beliefs. A layman typically accepts and believes evidence that a trained lawyer might not accept. A college-educated person is likely to have a different set of beliefs from those of an individual who has only a grade-school education. People with one religious background look at the world differently from individuals with a radically different religious background. Children will hold some beliefs in common with their parents but will also have beliefs that differ from those of their parents and grandparents. Women have beliefs that differ from those of men. Indeed, every individual differs from every other individual in some aspects of the nature and content of his belief system.

The definition of belief

Everyone has at least some meaning for the term **belief.** But a full discussion of the concept will enable us to use it precisely. In conversation, the term seems to be used in several ways. People talk about "believing in the Democratic Party," "believing in science," or "believing in the President of the United States." They also use the term to refer to the truth of a proposition or statement. People say, "I believe that we should have compulsory arbitration of labor disputes," "I believe that all Americans should be allowed to vote," or "I believe that this movie is the best one I have seen this year." These various statements seem to imply different uses of the term **belief.**

First, the term seems to be used in referring to an individual's **placing trust or confidence in a person or thing.** During the Depression of the 1930s, many Americans placed their trust in the abilities of Franklin D. Roosevelt. In the early 1960s, many citizens placed their trust in the late President Kennedy. They **believed** in him and were inclined to believe in the truth of any statement he made.

Second, to say that one believes in an individual seems to be different from **accepting a proposition as true.** All of us tend to accept or reject the statements we hear or read—whether about dating, animals, movies, food, labor disputes, or television. We also make and hear statements about politics, religion, history, science, and the future, and we say that we either **believe** or **disbelieve** in these statements.

A careful look at these two ways of describing beliefs discloses that although they appear to be different, they have much in common. To say that someone believes in a person is to say that he accepts a set of statements about the person as either true or false. For example, to say that a person "believes in the President of the United States" is to say that he accepts a set of statements about the President. The individual may accept the statements, "The President knows a lot about foreign relations," "The President is completely trustworthy," and "The President can really control Congress." The same individual is likely to reject the statements "The President is merely a politician," "The President has no sympathy for the working man," and "The President is soft on crime." All that the average individual knows about the President of the United States is the statements he reads or hears. He cannot know the man himself. He can know about the President's competence, trustworthiness, ability, and goodness only through a set of statements. Looking at the problem in this way, the basic definition of belief, whether in a person, thing, or idea, must be in terms of **accepting a proposition or statement as true.** This definition is an important one for the speaker to understand.

If a speaker is going to analyze an audience by looking at the beliefs its members hold, our definition suggests that he find out what statements they would accept as true. If he wishes to change the behavior or attitude of audience members, he must first find out what beliefs they hold and then be able to state the ways in which his proposed speech material differs from those beliefs. When a person writes a speech, the statements used in it will be related to the beliefs he holds, but one of his objectives will also be to make sure that the statements are related to the beliefs the audience holds. In this case, the speaker must be aware of both the statements he accepts as true and the statements the audience accepts as true.

Description of beliefs

In addition to simply defining the concept of belief, the speaker must also find some way of describing specific beliefs. Almost every statement an individual makes has at least some relation to a belief he holds, and it is not very useful to talk about beliefs in terms of the thousands of specific statements that might be made by a speaker. The speaker must be able to set up a system that will categorize beliefs.

The easiest way to categorize beliefs is in terms of the content of the belief statement. We can talk about statements referring to the population explosion, poverty, war, peace, education, and so forth. Each topic or content area may have many statements made about it;

for example, the communicator may say, "The population problem is more serious in India than in the United States," or "The population problem is bad and getting worse." These are two different statements made about the same content area.

The problem with categorizing beliefs in terms of the content area to which the statement is connected is that such a set of categories does not help us in making predictions about the receiver's possible reactions when he hears or reads a statement of belief. It can be of help in reducing the potential set of statements to more manageable size, but it does not help in making predictions about behavior. To assist the speaker in the latter task, we must turn to some predictions about the effects that beliefs have on our behavior.

One way of looking at beliefs is in terms of **belief–disbelief systems.** Individuals may hold a series of beliefs which are organized into systems of related beliefs. Individuals may also hold a series of disbeliefs, and these, too, may be organized into systems. Milton Rokeach, a psychologist who has written extensively about belief systems, suggests that individuals may have entire sets of belief–disbelief systems:

> The reader may note our use of the term **belief–disbelief system,** and possibly object that it sounds somewhat academic. Is not the disbelief system merely the mirror-image of the belief system, and thus unnecessary? Our own observations lead us to propose that this may not be the case. We will put forward the idea that every system is asymmetrical rather than symmetrical; it includes on the one hand a system of beliefs that one accepts, and on the other, a **series** of systems that one rejects.[2]

An individual may **believe** in the superiority of democracy, the necessity for birth control, freedom of speech, the usefulness of measles vaccine, and the power of the New York Mets. He may **disbelieve** in equality for blacks, the utility of divorce, drinking regulations for college students, and foreign aid. Disbelief is not a passive concept, and it is not merely the inversion of a belief. An individual may believe strongly in the necessity for birth control, but this does not mean that he will necessarily disbelieve in large families. He may disbelieve in foreign aid, but this does not mean that he believes in refusing to help foreign countries. The concepts an individual believes in may

[2] Milton Rokeach, **The Open and Closed Mind: Investigations into the Nature of Belief Systems and Personality Systems** (New York: Basic Books, 1960), p. 32.

have no seeming relationship to those he disbelieves in, and we are forced to discuss both the belief and disbelief systems of an individual.

Talking about the presence of belief–disbelief systems is not enough. The communicator must make some attempt at describing those systems in such a way that knowledge of them will be helpful to him in constructing messages. Rokeach suggests that each belief system is organized along a central–peripheral dimension. One set of beliefs is **central**, i.e., composed of beliefs that may be called **primitive** beliefs. These may be beliefs that the person has about the world around him, about religion, about the kinds of people the world contains, and, perhaps most important, about himself. These beliefs and disbeliefs are intensely held, normally formed early in the individual's life, and extremely difficult for the communicator to change. They can, however, be used as material to change less important beliefs.

The second level of beliefs is what Rokeach calls the **intermediate** region. This part of the belief–disbelief structure is concerned with an individual's beliefs about authorities. No one can hope to get all the information he needs to live and operate in the world from his own observations alone. He must depend on the opinions and reports of others. But we are all faced with the necessity of choosing between opposing authorities. Which authorities are chosen by an individual is a matter of belief, rather firmly held belief. Thus one individual may believe that if it "appears in the New York **Times**," it must be so. Another may believe that only television can give accurate news. One man may believe that only the President is really equipped to give the public the "facts," whereas another will believe that the government never tells a straight story. Older people today may place great faith in information given by the police, while younger individuals may refuse to believe in any statements issued by the police. The beliefs and disbeliefs held about authority are important for the speaker to assess in writing a message, because if he cites an authority that is likely to be disbelieved by his audience, the entire message is likely to be disbelieved.

The final level of the belief–disbelief structure is the **peripheral** region. Rokeach defines the peripheral level as containing those specific beliefs that are derived from central or intermediate beliefs. Examples of peripheral beliefs include: "I believe that the United States should extend its foreign-aid program," "The Beatles were the greatest rock group," and "Miniskirts are better than maxiskirts." Each of these is a specific belief linked to some central or intermediate belief. The individual may come to his belief about the foreign-aid program because he heard someone he respects make statements about the importance of foreign aid. Or he may believe very strongly in the "brotherhood of man" or in "helping your neighbor." If the speech communicator knows something about the intermediate and central beliefs of an individual, he can make predictions regarding the nature of that person's peripheral beliefs.

We may thus improve the quality of our predictions if we look more closely at the characteristics of beliefs as they fall within the central–peripheral dimension. But regardless of whether a belief is placed within the central, intermediate, or peripheral region, all beliefs may be characterized in terms of the **intensity** with which they are held and the **consistency** they exhibit.

Everyone has some beliefs that are seldom changed and are held with great intensity. An individual may believe very strongly that the United States has the best form of government in the world today. He may believe very strongly that the income tax should not be increased. He may believe that the Republican Party is the only party presenting a useful platform. These are beliefs that are held with high intensity. They will be difficult to change. But everyone also holds beliefs that are held with less intensity and may be easy to change. A person might believe that the school his son attends needs a new baseball diamond, but he does not really care much one way or the other. He might prefer one brand of beer but be willing to drink any other brand that is offered. Some beliefs are held very intensely, whereas other beliefs are held much less intensely.

To measure the beliefs an individual holds, first ascertain how interested he is in the general content area. For example, ask the individual whether he is interested in the topic "the population explosion." Ask whether he finds messages about the topic "interesting" or "uninteresting." To find out what his beliefs are toward a specific statement from the general content area, ask whether he "favors legislation to control the population explosion." You could get an even more precise answer from the respondent by asking him if he is "strongly in favor of," "moderately in favor of," "neutral toward," "moderately against," or "strongly against" such legislation.

The method suggested is one frequently used by the behavioral scientist to find out what beliefs and attitudes an individual holds. The speaker will find it useful to go one step further. It is helpful to know how an individual regards the major topic of one's speech. But it would be even more helpful to know how he feels about related topics. If an individual says he is in favor of legislation to help control the population explosion, the speaker might also wish to ask how he feels about birth control, income-tax deductions for dependents, job training, government food programs, emigration, and other topics that are related to the population problem. In other words, the speaker attempts to build up a picture of his auditor's entire belief structure. He will be interested in the intensity of the specific peripheral belief he may be attempting to change, but he will also be interested in those intermediate and central beliefs that may be associated with a particular peripheral belief.

Although the behavioral scientist is able to obtain fairly accurate information about the belief structures of the individuals he studies, the average speech communicator will not be able to obtain such direct evidence. He will be forced to make his predictions of what people will probably believe on the basis of those characteristics he can discover about the audience.

It is easier to find methods of estimating what the beliefs of a particular group of people are or are not if one realizes that beliefs are not held randomly. We have already suggested that beliefs are arranged into a hierarchical structure dependent on intensity of belief and nature of belief. We will be helped in understanding the belief structure of an individual if we realize that beliefs tend to be internally **consistent.** We do not expect an individual to believe both that capitalism is the best economic system and that the United States should elect a Communist government. We do not expect him to believe strongly in the separation of church and state and also believe that the government should sponsor prayers in the public schools. These would be inconsistent beliefs, and ordinarily our belief structure is arranged so that we do not hold beliefs that are inconsistent with one another.

Statements about the consistency of belief structures have to be qualified. For instance, an individual may hold two beliefs that seem to be inconsistent. If we probe carefully, however, we usually find that the individual has found some way to reconcile the apparent inconsistencies between his beliefs. Many people believe that smoking is related to lung cancer, yet they continue to smoke. If asked to explain this apparent inconsistency, they might suggest that to stop smoking makes them eat more, and that being overweight leads to high blood pressure and an increased chance of heart trouble. Another example might be the individual who states frequently that a particular brand of automobile is the best one on the market. If we see him driving a new car of a different make, we might be tempted to ask him about the inconsistency between his statements and his behavior. He may not see any inconsistency at all. His position may be that he does feel that the other brand of car is better, but that he "got a better deal" on this brand. Or he may claim that his wife really made the choice of the car he is driving. People use many ways to explain the beliefs they hold and the behaviors they exhibit. The one thing we may be sure of is that they will try to use explanations that "make sense" to them, although they may not make sense to anyone else.

In describing beliefs, the communicator may assess the specific nature of a belief in terms of the content area to which it refers. He may also make some assessment of the intensity with which it is held. And finally, he may describe the belief in terms of a belief–disbelief structure and perhaps assign it to a central, intermediate, or peripheral region within the belief structure of the individual.

Prediction of beliefs

The reader who is interested in proving his case or in constructing a speech designed to persuade an audience may well complain at this point that although he thinks the discussion interesting, he needs help in finding out what the beliefs of his audience are. The normal speaker is not a behavioral scientist, nor can he pass out tests before his speech in order to ascertain what beliefs his audience holds. Moreover, when he is sitting in a study attempting to compose a speech, it is difficult to make predictions about the audience he will be facing. Indeed, the complexity of people would seem to point to the impossibility of ever finding out, in anything more than the most superficial fashion, what any group of individuals believes.

Before attempting to help the communicator with this problem, let us point out that he will probably never be able to detail completely the beliefs his audience holds. But predictions can be made about the belief–disbelief systems of an audience that will be more helpful in constructing the message to be delivered than operating without any knowledge of the audience at all.

The communicator usually faces an audience composed of individuals whom he has met only casually if at all. He may have only general information about the audience. For example, a communicator who is delivering a speech to an audience interested in Peace Corps training might know that the members of the audience are drawn from a university community and that they are interested in the Peace Corps, but he probably knows no more than that. In another case, a speaker might be addressing a group interested in hospital care. The group might be drawn from all over the community, but except for their presumed interest in the functions of a hospital, he might know nothing about the related opinions, attitudes, and information levels of the audience.

Although communicators may never hope to make a complete analysis of their audience, they should at least attempt to make **some** predictions of the beliefs that a particular audience is likely to have. To make this kind of analysis, the speaker must **infer** what kinds of beliefs are held by his auditors. For example, let us suppose that a communicator is speaking to a PTA group at a local school anywhere in the United States. He has available to him a tremendous amount of information about the general nature of his audience if he can think about the problem for a short time. He knows that his listeners are going to be interested in and have beliefs about children. He can guess that there are likely to be more women than men present, because more women attend PTA meetings than do men. He knows that this group is likely to represent the so-called middle-class population of the United States because schools of the very wealthy and of the very poor are not likely to have organized PTA groups that plan programs with speakers. If he knows the city and the locality within the city, a two-minute drive in areas around the school may tell him that this is a suburban group, or an urban group. He may see a large factory close to the school that will tell him something else about the probable socioeconomic background of the group. Talking to the chairman or chairwoman for just a few minutes before the program starts may help the speaker avoid certain errors. He might thus find out that this group in general comes from a particular nationality background or that they all have common occupational backgrounds.

Once the speaker has information about the group, he must find some way of using that information to predict the kinds of beliefs or disbeliefs the group is likely to have. For example, an audience having children of school age is likely to be sensitive to and hold specific beliefs regarding new health treatments for children's diseases. A group of factory employees may be expected to have favorable beliefs regarding labor unions. A group of young, suburban couples who are buying their own homes may well have unfavorable beliefs about the value of additional property taxes for financing schools. Conversely, a group living in apartments may well favor the property tax over the income tax as a way of financing schools.

Each of these "guesses" about the beliefs of a particular group are **inferences**—inferences about the beliefs the group holds made from data gathered without asking a single question about an individual's beliefs. As we pointed out in the first chapter, such inferences could be wrong, and in attempting to predict what a particular belief might be from other characteristics, the communicator may draw an incorrect conclusion. We should also point out, however, that making the attempt is usually better than not taking beliefs into account at all.

There are many characteristics indicating the beliefs we hold. For the speech communicator, however, **group membership** is probably the most important characteristic to ascertain. The kinds of groups we belong to, while not providing an infallible indicator of beliefs held, may help in making that determination. People who have children are more likely to favor increased support for public schools in the community than will people who do not have children. Thus, this group membership, i.e., having children, becomes a predictor of certain attitudes. Some of the characteristics of groups that the communicator can usually obtain specific information about include the following:

1. The interests of individuals change with the **age** of the individual. Speaking to a teenage audience is certainly different from speaking to an audience of young married people or of retired couples. The average age of an audience may tell a great deal about the kinds of beliefs individual audience members are likely to have and about the interests, attitudes, and opinions they might be expected to express. One might object to this generalization by saying that, after all, most audiences are spread across many different ages, and thus average age would not be a very good predictor. Experience tells us, however, that this spread of age seldom happens in speech commu-

nication situations. Most audiences have a fairly narrow range of ages or are composed of two different age ranges. A speaker is most likely to be talking to groups of children, teenagers, young married couples, older married couples, and so on until he reaches groups of individuals in their "golden years." He may also face audiences that are mixed between two age groups, such as fathers and sons. The average age of the audience does provide an indicator of the nature of the experiences its members may have had and thus gives some indication of the beliefs they may hold. For example, an individual who lived as a young adult during the Great Depression of the 1930s may well have strong beliefs about the value of saving money that someone born during the 1950s will not have.

2. Many of the activities that people engage in happen in groups of men alone or women alone. Women brought together for a garden-club meeting may be expected to have a different set of expectations from those of a group of men brought together for a hunting-club meeting. The **sex** of particular audiences is another variable that may help the communicator in identifying beliefs. Most of us would agree that men and women may hold similar sets of beliefs, but when men and women are in different social groupings, the beliefs that are uppermost will differ, and the speaker should take account of those differences. The woman attending a meeting of her sorority will be thinking of different things, and thus be susceptible to different messages, from the man attending a meeting of his lodge. The beliefs that the communicator uses to elicit beliefs, as well as the beliefs that he might expect to change, will differ with the sex of his listeners. When an audience is composed of either men alone or women alone, these sex-related beliefs will be intensified.

3. That it is valid to suggest that different **ethnic and nationality groups** will hold different sets of beliefs has been demonstrated again and again. For example, a recent item in the newspaper indicated how German and American doctors differ in their beliefs regarding pregnancy. The article mentioned that German doctors do not urge the mother-to-be to drink milk but encourage her to drink light wines. Such a difference could be repeated again and again in examples from all over the world. This variable may seem of little help to the speaker in the United States, where ethnic and nationality groups have all become mixed into a common culture. It is certainly the case that we have a relatively common culture in the United States, and we

do not expect people in Seattle to differ greatly in many of their beliefs from those in Detroit or Miami. Nevertheless, almost all of us have a nationality identification of some type, and many of us are extremely proud of that identification. We may have English, German, Japanese, Indian, or Italian grandparents or great-grandparents. We may be black, white, or brown. Although all are American, most families retain some practices and beliefs that tie them to the "old country." Our race may mean that we will have certain views of the world and of ourselves. In many areas, both within the city and in rural communities, these ties are strong, and the speaker who does not take them into account will not be successful. In Michigan, for example, there is a very strong Polish community living in a Detroit suburb. Many of the citizens still speak Polish at home, there is a Polish-language newspaper, and the smells of Polish cooking fill the air. Former Governor G. Mennen Williams, a four-time winner of the gubernatorial chair, knew a great deal about the ideas and practices of these citizens, and much of his success may be traced to his ability to adapt to the ideas and beliefs of this and other nationality groups that make up the pluralistic society of the state of Michigan.

4. A few years ago, people could be separated very easily on the basis of the **level of education** they had attained. Relatively few Americans had the opportunity to obtain more than a high-school education, and many millions more could show only an eighth-grade diploma. The beliefs and disbeliefs of people with relatively little education seemed to differ greatly from those of college-educated individuals. In particular, the central and intermediate beliefs of college graduates were significantly different from those of persons with relatively little education.

Today the picture has changed somewhat. More and more children go on to college, and almost all children obtain at least some portion of a high-school education. At all levels, children get a more uniform education. This means that differences in belief systems because of differences in education will be less dramatic. However, there are still differences, and these need to be taken into account by the communicator. There are educational differences depending on whether a child went to school in the inner city, a suburb, or a rural area. There will be differences between the college student who attends a large, public state university and the college man who attends a small, private university. An audience composed of college graduates will have had different experiences, and thus hold different beliefs, from an audience composed of individuals who never attended college. The communicator may find that peripheral beliefs do not differ dramatically, but beliefs about authority and about the nature of the physical world may differ radically with the educational level of the audience.

5. An individual's **occupation** determines many of his beliefs. A social worker who works daily with juvenile delinquents, for example, is likely to have different beliefs about the treatment of teenagers than a farmer who seldom sees a juvenile delinquent. The factory worker, operating a lathe in a machine shop, is likely to have a different set of beliefs about the treatment of the laborer than a company accountant who never enters the plant.

In many respects, occupation is the best predictor of belief–disbelief systems that the communicator has available to him. Unfortunately, except for the relatively rare situation in which the speaker knows he is addressing a group from the same occupational class, he is unable to make maximum use of this predictor of belief, because his audience will consist of people from many different occupations. When it is possible, however, a careful look at what an occupation entails about the possible belief systems of an individual holding that occupation will be extremely useful to the communicator.

6. The **political preference** variable is not useful in all situations. Furthermore, in the United States, the two major political parties do not differ so drastically that we may expect the central or intermediate belief systems to be very much different for a Republican than for a Democrat. However, there are specific peripheral beliefs on which the Republican Party will differ from the Democratic Party. If a communicator should be speaking to an audience with a majority of active members of a single party, he should take this knowledge into account in predicting beliefs. For example, Democrats in general might be expected to favor a graduated state income tax over a flat-rate income tax. Democrats might also be expected to favor federal aid to education, and federal enactment of social legislation. Republicans might be expected to favor more state control of projects, more freedom for business to operate, and more control of welfare projects.

In spite of the fact that there are relatively few major differences between the two major political parties, a speech communicator may find help in the knowledge that there are many smaller political groups in the United States. The American Independent Party, developed by George Wallace for the 1968 campaign, represents a set of beliefs considerably different from those of either of the two major parties. The Conservative Party in New York and some of the small radical parties of the Left also represent political positions that the communicator may be able to use to advantage.

7. **Religion** is very much like political preference as a predictive variable. It certainly is a predictor of some beliefs, but it is difficult to ascertain exactly what the religious composition of an audience is. When a speaker knows his audience is composed entirely of Lutherans or Roman Catholics or Methodists, he may look to the causes these groups espouse and to the principles they profess as predictors of their probable beliefs. But when the audience is mixed, as it more frequently is, the best he can do with this variable is to attempt to ascertain whether his audience is composed primarily of Christians or of individuals from another major religious group. He may then estimate the probable beliefs of the majority of the audience. Even then, the religion of a listener is more likely to be reflected in the central way in which he views the world or the nature of the authorities he accepts as valid than in the specific beliefs or disbeliefs to which the speaker is addressing his remarks.

8. A final variable that may help a communicator predict the beliefs of his audience is that of **organizational membership.** Most people belong to several organizations. They may be members of a country club, a bowling league, an alumni member of some fraternity, a civic organization, a gourmet cooking club, or a garden club. Speakers will frequently find themselves addressing an audience that has a high preponderance of members of a specific organization. When a speaker knows that many members of an audience are also members of the Elks Club, for instance, he may use this fact to help predict the beliefs that audience holds. In this example, he may be able to find out what the Elks project for the year is, and use this information to make predictions and compose messages relative to that project.

There are other variables that might help in predicting the belief structures of listeners, but the ones that have been discussed are certainly the most helpful. One further point should be mentioned, however. The situation in which a listener is participating probably has a great deal to do with his reaction to any speech. When an individual is meeting with members of his bowling club to hear a speech, his interest in bowling is probably of more immediate importance in identifying his belief structure than the fact that he is also a Republican and a Methodist. The fact that audience members belong to a hospital auxiliary group meeting at a hospital to hear a speech calling for additional tax funds for hospital services is probably more important to the speaker in determining the beliefs of that audience than the fact that some of them are Roman Catholics or have college educations. In other words, peripheral beliefs in any specific situation may change somewhat depending on the other people present and the nature of the situation itself.

Summary

This chapter concentrated on belief and disbelief as concepts important to understanding the concept of proof and on the role belief plays in oral communication. The speaker must know what his own beliefs are and what beliefs he is interested in establishing or modifying in his audience. The speaker must also be able to use the beliefs of his audience to secure belief from that audience.

In describing beliefs, we said that beliefs and disbeliefs are not held randomly by audience members. They are organized systematically into belief–disbelief patterns on central, intermediate, and peripheral levels. They may be described in terms of their content and the intensity with which they are held.

Finally, the chapter looked at a number of variables that the speaker may investigate in trying to predict the beliefs of an audience, so that he may use the concept of belief in establishing materials that will help him prove his case.

THREE

Belief and the process of communication

Analyzing beliefs, his own and those of his audience, helps the communicator in preparing his materials. A typical audience analysis will usually show a mixture of attitudes—some members will already be favorable toward the speaker's position, and others will be either neutral or negative. The communicator may find it strange that a large percentage of the individuals in any audience are not in agreement with him on any topic, even though they seem to have access to the same background information. He may ask, "Why do different people develop different beliefs? How does it happen that two people can look at the same set of events and come to two different conclusions regarding those events? What kind of changes in belief or attitudes can I ever expect to secure from my audience? What role does the nature of our society play in determining the nature of communication?" This chapter concentrates on these and similar questions to provide a basis for the emphasis on types of evidence to be discussed in the rest of the book.

A model for human communication

The speech communication process is often taken for granted. We learn to speak at so early an age that we never ask what is involved in speech communication. The process can be described in many different ways, depending on the purpose in looking at the process. More than forty different descriptions of the communication process have appeared in print in various places, some of them more than two thousand years old. Writers have differed in their conception of the process, depending on the importance they attach to various levels of the communication process. One writer may confine himself to the social aspects of the communication process, another to the role played by the mass media in the process, and a third to the psychological principles involved in oral communication. In this volume, the interest is in proof and in building a model of the communication process relevant to the study of the concept of proof. We have already indicated that oral communication depends on the ability of a communicator to utilize evidence to induce belief in an audience. Thus, any model of communication we utilize must attempt to explain how we can change an individual's beliefs, attitudes, and behaviors through the presentation of evidence in an oral communication situation. The analysis, however, must take place at several levels because it is extremely difficult to talk about the process of communication as a whole without breaking it down into several subprocesses.

An observer able to hide behind a one-way mirror and watch two people engaged in conversation might listen to that conversation and then attempt to make a diagram of what was happening. Gathering his data, he might include a speaker, a listener, and a set of messages as the essential elements in the situation. If he listens a bit longer, questions might occur to him about this initial formulation. He might wonder where the speaker is getting the materials he is talking about. He might be concerned about the fact that the listener does not seem to be in immediate agreement with the speaker. He might notice that the listener does not seem to be making very many responses. He might conclude that the speaker was being unsuccessful in his efforts. If the observer were very perceptive, he might notice that both the speaker and the listener have certain behaviors that they seem to hold in common as well as certain behaviors about which they seem to differ. Eventually he would attempt his diagram.

One such attempt at modeling the communication process is shown in Figure 1. We cannot include all possible elements within a single diagram. Figure 1, however, does detail some of the more important ingredients in the communication process. The model shown in Figure 1 is an adaptation of some ideas about communication first

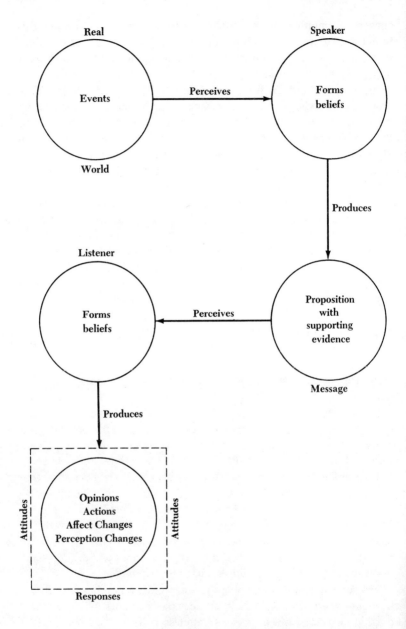

Figure 1. The Oral Communication Process

advanced by Dean George Gerbner of the University of Pennsylvania.[1] It suggests that in any oral communication situation there is a SPEAKER who PERCEIVES an event or series of events in the REAL WORLD and then develops a BELIEF about those events. He next PRODUCES a MESSAGE about his beliefs by organizing evidence around a proposition and transmits that message to a LISTENER or a group of LISTENERS who PERCEIVE the MESSAGE and take some position of BELIEF toward it. That position is indicated when the listener PRODUCES a RESPONSE to the message.

This basic process is found in all communication situations. Sometimes the process will be complicated by the presence of more than one listener or more than one speaker. Sometimes it will be complicated by having the message sent over radio or television or printed in a newspaper. Sometimes the speaker will be separated in time or space from the receiver. But regardless of the variations that occur, the basic process of communication must occur much as it is diagrammed in Figure 1.

A look at this model of the communication process indicates that there are at least two common processes shared by source and receiver. Both source and receiver are engaged in the process of **perception,** the process by which we are made aware of the world around us. Both source and receiver **produce** responses to the stimuli which they perceive. The close examination of these processes of **perception** and **production** is the goal of the remainder of this chapter.

Perception: becoming aware of the world

People are constantly being made aware of the events around them. From the time when, as new-born babies, we first notice a sound through all of our adult years, we are engaged in perceiving events. In communication, our eyes and ears bear the primary responsibility for giving us information about the world, although the other senses of taste, touch, smell, balance, and kinesthetics also play a part in the perception process.

Our world is so rich in available stimuli that a single individual cannot possibly respond to all the stimuli around him at any given time. The source who is gathering information for a speech may notice

[1] George Gerbner, "Toward a General Model of Communication," **Audio-Visual Communication Review,** 4 (Summer 1956), 171–199.

only a small portion of the events that make up the world around him. If he is watching a busy street in preparation for a speech on traffic conditions in the city, he may be aware of the cars as they pass by his position and of the changing traffic lights as they regulate the flow of traffic. He may not perceive the pedestrians crossing against the light or the buildings across the street. A reporter sitting down to write a story about a fire may be aware of only a few of the events occurring around him. He does not notice the radio playing in the next office or the roar of the presses downstairs. A listener, also, cannot respond to all available stimuli. He may see and hear a speaker delivering his speech, but he does not respond to a light flickering overhead or the feel of the chair underneath him or the movements of the person sitting behind him. People are capable of perceiving the world around them, but they also possess a built-in mechanism for choosing only those elements of the situation that seem most important at a particular time.

It is this selective process that makes individuals arrive at different conclusions about the same event, even though they view the same event at the same time and from the same vantage point. Thus, if a group of people all view an attempted robbery and then try to describe what happened, one person may have attended to the suspect's clothes, another to the weapon he used, a third to the words he said, and a fourth to the condition of the victim. None would be able to report on the complete scene, even after looking at the situation several times. Similarly, one listener, seated in an auditorium listening to a speech, might well come away from the situation with completely different impressions of the speech and the speaker from those of the individual seated next to him.

In another situation, a group of people might observe several children coming home from school. One person concentrates on the child who runs across a lawn and mutters something about "young hoodlums." Another perceives two boys scuffling and begins to worry about the school's failure to exercise control. A third looks at the dresses of the girls and comments on the probable income of their parents. If the three individuals were later to use their perceptions of the event as evidence in a speech, it might well sound as if the three had observed three different events. Each person has observed essentially the same scene, but each person has selected from that scene what seems important to **him**, and his beliefs and actions reflect what he has perceived.

In Chapter 2, we looked at some of the bases for belief. Now we should note that people have different beliefs in part because they perceive different portions of events. Conversely people select different portions of an event to perceive, in part because they have different beliefs. The process of perception and the process of belief are closely intertwined. In our model of communication, both source and receiver are affected by their beliefs when they perceive events and produce responses to their perceptions.

It is clear that we cannot experience directly the daily life of an individual living in another city or country. We will not have exactly the same beliefs as someone from another country, or another city, or even the same city. Actually, even when we are all looking at the same event, different beliefs may result from our perception because we are all motivated differently. What gets in, via the perceptual process, is in part determined by personal internal states. There are many such internal states, some biologic in nature and some that have been acquired by experience. Only a few are discussed below, but they are enough to indicate how widely differing beliefs may be developed and thus, how selective perception may occur.

If I am hungry, I am likely to select and concentrate on events in the perceptual world that might lead to food. I will be more attracted to pictures of food, the smells of cooking, or the sound of the dinner bell. After eating, I may completely pass over a picture of a juicy steak in a magazine, and if asked whether I saw the picture, I might say no. Hunger is only one **biologic motive,** or **drive.** Others include **thirst, pain avoidance,** and **sex.** These biologic drives may not be as important in communication as some that are learned, but they are powerful indicators of what is perceived, and thus of what is believed, by an individual. A listener forced to sit in an uncomfortable chair when listening to a speech will retain a different impression of the speech than will his neighbor who sits in a comfortable chair. The receiver who listens to a speech immediately after dinner will perceive, and believe, differently than will the receiver who listens on an empty stomach. Biologic drives do help in determining the nature of what is perceived and retained by receivers.

Every child, regardless of his nationality, spends a lot of his time in learning to value certain behaviors. For example, a child may be taught that he has a duty to be loyal to his country. When he grows up, this may lead to his volunteering for military service when he hears a speech in which the speaker appeals to the motive of loyalty. Or a child may hear certain comments about the traditional customs of his family. He may grow up to place high value on conformity and would respond favorably to speech materials attempting to support a proposition by referring to what people thought in the past or to what family custom demands.

There are many **learned motives,** and from them we learn the nature of the culture in which we live, what life is like, and the stimuli to which we will respond. Common learned motives in the United States include desires for social participation, honor, loyalty, competition, and conformity. In other cultures, the strength of the competition motive, for example, may not be as strong as it is in the United States, and a speaker would have to emphasize different motives in order to be a successful communicator.

Neither biologic nor learned motives operate within a vacuum. The diagram we have utilized and the examples we have cited might lead to the conclusion that the source and the receiver perceive in isolation from other sources and receivers. The diagram does not indicate the many other factors that help determine the nature of the communication that takes place, the constraints placed on the communication situation itself, or the role that other sources of communication play in determining the effects of communication.

Speech communication may take place under many circumstances: a chat across the back fence with a neighbor, a few comments over a cup of coffee with a friend in a restaurant, casual remarks at a Girl Scout committee, a formal speech at a national convention, a nationwide address of the President over all possible types of mass media. Most people do not engage in nationwide addresses or even in speeches to national conventions. But they do speak to their neighbors, and they probably make some remarks to the social and civic groups to which they belong. Perhaps more important than the speaking they do, however, is the listening they do. In a very real sense, it is that listening that determines what they will believe and say in future situations.

To suggest that communication can take place in many different types of situations is to suggest that the **social situation** in which communication occurs is a variable important to the speaker's success. What an individual might be willing to do or believe in one situation is not what he would be willing to believe or do in another situation. When one is alone with a speaker, it is sometimes easier to respond to his statements than when one is seated in the middle of a large auditorium surrounded by many other people. It is easier to perceive selectively when one is in isolation than when communication must take place among many competing stimuli. A very good example of the constraints a social situation may place on a listener is the political rally that includes a number of hecklers. Even though the average listener wants to concentrate on the speaker, the presence of competing stimuli being produced by the hecklers may make it impossible for him actually to perceive much of what the speaker is saying. The social situation, then, may serve to modify the effects of both biologic and learned motives in the perception process.

This section concentrated on the bases for perception by both speaker and receiver. Our communication model indicates that the speaker gets his information through the process of perception and that information may be modified by the presence of biologic motives, learned motives, and the nature of the social situation.

Production: responding to the world

Psychologists are fond of saying that when a stimulus has been perceived by an individual, a response will follow. In our diagram, we have noted that the process of **production** applies to both source and receiver. The source perceives the real world, integrates what he perceives according to the operation of biologic and learned motives, and makes a response that we term the **message.** The message that he produces, both the verbal and nonverbal aspects of it, must be perceived by the listener before he can make a response to it. Here, however, we frequently seem to have a problem. We can all notice the effect of the speaker's perception of the world around him since it results in the production of a message. But a speaker is frequently faced with the situation in which his speech has been made without a discernible reaction from the audience. Has he failed in his purpose? Does the audience not perceive the message? Not necessarily. Figure 1 notes that there are at least four types of response that the listener may make to any message: **opinion** changes, **perception** changes, **affect** changes, and **action** changes. Some of these changes are easily observed by the speaker; others are not so easily observed.

Opinion changes may be defined as changes in what an individual says after a speech. An individual might say, "I have been wrong. I

agree with the speaker that we need a new foreign policy." This statement represents some change in opinion on the part of the listener.
Opinion changes are changes in the way the individual verbalizes his
beliefs and values. For many speech situations, the source must
depend on such opinion statements as the only indication he will
receive about the success of his speech.

One situation is the case in which the listener receives a message,
and his response is to encode a response to it **that is also a message
then received by the source.** The receiver might say, "I'm sorry, but I
don't understand what you are trying to say," or "I don't think you are
right," or "I can only agree with part of what you have said." In this
situation, the message encoded by the listener does represent an
opinion change on his part, but it also serves as **feedback** to the
source about the degree of success of his message. Such interpersonal situations are quite common, and the importance of feedback
in the speech communication situation cannot be overstated. Feedback may serve to stimulate further messages and responses from
the source of the original message, and the situation truly becomes
one of a process occurring over time.

A **perception change** occurs when the receiver changes the way in
which he perceives a problem. For example, imagine someone listening to a speech on the plight of the American Indian. He may leave
the speech situation and later look at the next Indian he sees not as
the derelict he formerly saw but simply as an individual less fortunate
than himself. Or take the individual who detests long hair on men. If
he approves of what a speaker is saying, he may go away from the
speech not even noticing that the speaker has long hair. Perception
changes are difficult for the source to detect. There may be no observable change in an individual's behavior. But the speech may still
have had some effect, because the individual has changed the way in
which he views the world. There has been a perception change.

Affect changes are changes in the emotional state of the listener.
There is probably nothing more difficult to define or detect than a
change in an individual's emotional state. Nevertheless, many listeners do experience a change in feeling toward a speaker as they are
listening to a speech—a change in sympathy for him or dislike for
him. These emotional changes may then become reflected in changes
of opinion or attitude toward the topic of the speaker's message. As
difficult as they are to detect, affect changes are responses to stimuli,

and they may affect the production of messages on the part of a source or be the produced response on the part of a receiver.

Finally, we may look at **action changes**—clear changes in overt, observable behavior. The listener reaches into his pocket to donate money to the speaker's cause. Or he goes into the voting booth to vote for the candidate favored by the communicator. Imagine a listener exposed to a speech on the population problem. He listens, and as a result of the speech he now begins reading every article he can find on the subject. He may say nothing about the speech, nor does he rush out to offer money or help to the cause. But his new reading habits represent an action change and further indicate that the speech has had some effect.

The four types of response that individuals produce as a result of their perceptions of the world or of messages all take place against a pattern of attitude change on the part of the source or receiver. We hypothesize that when some observable change takes place, the change cannot take place before there has been a corresponding attitude change. We cannot see when an individual has changed his attitude, because attitudes are nonobservable. But when one of the observable changes we have discussed takes place, this means that an attitude change has occurred. It is possible, however, for an attitude change to take place that is not followed by a **detectable** change in opinions, perceptions, emotions, or actions.

From a consideration of attitude changes of varying degrees, the process can be traced by which an individual decides to adopt a new idea that has been presented to him. This process entails five steps: **attention, interest, trial, evaluation,** and **adoption.**

For any communicator to be successful, he must first have the **attention** of the people to whom he is talking. To achieve this, he will have to present materials that give the listener a reason for listening. He has to appeal to some internal biologic or learned motive that the listener holds and make the listener select his particular message. In the "captive audience" situation, where the speaker does not have competing stimuli to contend with, securing at least some minimum degree of attention may not be difficult. But in a mass media situation, where the source's message is in competition with many other competing stimuli, the problem of securing attention may be a very difficult one. When there are thirteen channels on the television set, getting a listener to select one channel over another requires careful preparation of materials that will give the receiver some reason for staying on one channel rather than switching.

The second step in successful communication, more difficult than the first, is arousing **interest** in the problem under discussion. Many of us have spent time listening to a speech, and actually attended to the content of the speech, but have left the situation with little real interest in what the speaker was saying. Again, the speaker will need to provide enough evidence and utilize enough appeals to induce the listener to feel that he should be interested and concerned about the problem. Attention and interest go hand in hand, and they are generally the easiest reactions to secure from an audience in an oral communication situation. However, many communicators make the mistake of assuming that they have been successful in accomplishing specific changes in behavior when they have only succeeded in getting auditors to show that they have paid attention and are interested in the material. Most of us can remember situations and speakers who got us interested but not to the extent of doing anything about the problem. Attention and interest are prerequisites to successful communication, but they are not the entire story.

The last three steps, while originally suggested by scholars interested in the diffusion of new ideas, actually fit most communication situations where proof is involved. **Trial, evaluation,** and **adoption** are more difficult to accomplish than are attention and interest, but they are equally important. After the speaker has people interested in the new topic or new idea he is espousing, he may need to add more information, more appeals, and more evidence to the materials of his message in order to get the receivers to try the new idea or to consider acceptance of a proposition. The receiver may be interested in something new, but if a trial will require particular efforts or monetary expenditures, the level of proof required of the communicator must be higher than that used to get the listener's attention or interest.

Assuming that the speaker has been successful in getting a listener to try an idea or topic once—"try it on for size"—he must also communicate the necessity of making some evaluation of the trial. Again, the communicator may have to include possible criteria, standards, and methods for evaluation. If one gets a farmer to plant some new bean variety, he must then show the farmer how to compare the old variety with the new variety. If a speaker advocates support for a challenger in a political campaign, he must include methods by which the listener can evaluate the relative merits of the challenger and the incumbent. Receivers are always evaluating the ideas they hear and the topics they are exposed to. They will use their own methods of evaluation unless the communicator can supply them with better methods.

Finally, assuming that an individual has made an evaluation that favors the new idea, further communication may be necessary in order to convince him that adoption of the idea on a permanent basis will be helpful to him. Many individuals "know what is good for them" but may cling to old habits and ideas out of simple unwillingness to abandon them, even in the face of a trial and successful evaluation of that trial. Additional motivation and additional materials may need to be fed them on a continuing basis if they are to adopt a new idea permanently.

In studying the perception process, we noted that the social situation in which communication takes place is an important element in determining what will be perceived. The social situation is equally important in determining what responses will be produced by speakers and listeners. A very good example of the constraints that a social situation may place on a listener is the typical response to the speaker's request, "Does anyone have any questions?" Many of us have sat in an auditorium and watched a group of people respond to that question by saying nothing. The speaker might well feel that his message was completely understood. However, it is more likely that the presence of a large group of people has inhibited an individual from asking questions—particularly from asking what he may feel is a "stupid question." Watch what happens after the speech. Frequently, individuals will come up to the speaker and **then** begin asking questions. The presence of other people in the oral communication situation does place some social constraints on the types of responses that are likely to be made.

Constraints work in more than one way, however. It is sometimes easier for a listener to say no when he and the speaker are alone than when they are joined by other people and the listener feels social pressure to take the action recommended by the speaker. Many of us have had the experience of being asked to help with some civic project. If we were asked during a meeting at which other members of the association were present, it was difficult to say no. Even though we would have experienced no punishments nor been ostracized from the group, we felt pressure to do what had been asked. On the other hand, if the same request were made of us, phrased in exactly the same words, in a telephoned message, the social pressure would be largely gone. We can say no to requests in the absence of social pressure to which we might respond positively in the presence of perceived social pressure.

The source must analyze the nature of the social situation in which he is operating just as he analyzes the nature of the individuals who are in the situation. Sources are constrained in what they may say and how they say it by the nature of the social situation. Similarly, receivers are constrained in how they respond by the nature of the social situation. A failure to realize that people will not take certain kinds of suggestions because of the nature of the social situation can mean a failure of the communicator to accomplish his intent. It is always difficult to generalize about what responses to expect, but a few hypotheses may be made:

1. When there is social pressure that tends to operate contrary to a speaker's intent, the presence of a group is likely to be inhibiting to the speaker.

2. When a speaker is advocating a position that is in line with the majority of the audience's thinking, the presence of the audience will tend to facilitate the speaker's purpose and bring dissenting members into line.

3. When the intent of the speaker is to produce action on the part of individual audience members, the presence of the audience may help to reduce the pressures that would normally lead one to refuse to respond positively.

4. When the speaker's intent is to change attitudes in a direction away from the commonly accepted norms for a proposition, the presence of an audience that **shows agreement** with the speaker will facilitate audience acceptance of such change. On the other hand, if the audience does not show agreement in some way, the production of response is inhibited for those members of the audience who might tend to agree with the speaker. (This is why "ringers" or "shills" are sometimes placed in an audience to show agreement with the speaker and thus lead others to agree with him.)

5. A speaker who intends to obtain a response that merely indicates agreement with his position is perhaps more likely to secure it when only one receiver is present. But a positive response to a request for

specific action may be easier to secure when other audience members are also agreeing to take similar actions.

These five propositions describe only a few of the situations that a speaker may encounter. But they serve to indicate the importance of the social situation on the production of responses in oral communication situations. A speaker's attempt to provide proof for his propositions may depend on the nature of the social situation as well as on the type of response that is desired. He may secure responses in a church that cannot be secured at a Kiwanis luncheon. He may secure responses when he has the listener alone that would be difficult to obtain when he is facing the same listener in a large group of other listeners. The speaker must make as careful an analysis of the social situation in which communication is taking place as he does of the other elements of the situation.

Summary

This chapter examined the relationship between belief and the oral communication process. The model of communication we examined points to the crucial importance of the processes of perception and production of response for both the source and the receiver. The creation of beliefs is partially dependent on the nature of the perceptual process, which was described as selective in nature and dependent on the needs, desires, memories, and past experiences of the source and the receiver. The production of responses by source and receiver is constrained by the attitudes they hold, which then help determine potential changes in opinions, perceptions, emotions, or actions. A hierarchy of responses in terms of difficulty of achievement by the source was suggested, indicating that the hierarchy ranged from attention and interest to trial, evaluation, and adoption. The importance of the nature of the social situation to both perception and production was emphasized, and the relationships between the nature of the social situation and the difficulty of the speaker's task was discussed. To conclude, the nature of the evidence needed by a speaker to prove his case and the amount of that evidence needed are determined in large part by the kind of response desired and the situation in which it is desired.

FOUR

Substantive proof: evidence

One of the most interesting characteristics of people is their eagerness to transmit their ideas to other people. Think over the last two-
or three-day period and ask yourself how many times you talked to
someone else about an idea you had. How many times did you listen
to someone else talk about an idea he had? Whether you are speaking
or listening, communication is concerned with ideas, i.e., with those
pieces of information used to generate thought. Proposals, suggestions, notions, theses, and advice are all terms we use to refer to those
ideas that are the basis for the messages you send or receive. The
problem is that such ideas or information may or may not actually
support the source's intentions.

Imagine two teenage boys talking together. One boy is trying to
convince the other that they should steal a car to go see their girl
friends. The evidence he offers in support of his idea is, "No one will
see us, and we can get the car back in an hour." The friend finally
agrees, and shortly after driving away with the "borrowed" automobile,
the police stop the two boys for a traffic violation. Here is a situation
where the idea proved not to be a good idea; that is, the consequences
of putting the idea into operation proved undesirable. More careful
exploration of those consequences by both the source and the receiver might have meant that the idea would not have been adopted.

The first chapter of this book, in defining proof as the process of using evidence to test ideas, did not stress that ideas must be tested in two ways within the typical oral communication situation. The communicator who gets an idea must test the adequacy of that idea before he transmits it. The auditors must test the idea again through their evaluation of the evidence presented by the communicator. The following discussion of various modes of proof has two values. It is concerned with the ways in which the communicator arrives at a position on matters of public policy. And it is concerned with the ways in which a communicator might present his position to an audience so that they, too, will be more likely to arrive at the same position.

A concept of evidence

It might seem relatively easy to discuss evidence from the standpoint of both the speaker and his audience. An example points out some of the problems. In the United States today, a number of people claim to have seen "spaceships" land and to have seen "small green men" emerge from the spaceships. Some have even claimed to have talked to the "small green men" and to have ridden into space in the spaceships. These people have told others about their experiences, and been disbelieved. Why have they been disbelieved? After all, they are presenting evidence for their views, purportedly the evidence of their own eyes. Many of these people seem quite sincere in their statements that they have seen the objects and the people they describe. But when they report their experiences to others, they are not believed. What was proof for the communicator was not proof for the receiver.

Spaceships and little green men comprise an extreme example of the problem that plagues every court of law and every policy maker in any legislature. What does constitute adequate evidence for the support of any proposition? What kind of evidence is necessary to satisfy every member of an audience? In one sense, these questions can never be answered. It is probably impossible to set up proof for any proposition in such a way that every possible auditor will accept the proposition. Even in a case as well documented as the assassination of President Kennedy, there remains a small group of people who vehemently maintain that Lee Harvey Oswald was not the individual who fired the murder weapon. They are not satisfied with the evidence offered to support the main proposition.

Any classification of evidence that we use must be qualified, because proof is related to belief. Therefore, it may be impossible to ever "prove" our case to the satisfaction of every auditor. In general, the more the auditor is likely already to agree with the communicator, the less evidence is needed. In the case of the spaceships, most auditors find the proposition to be one that is completely foreign to them. They will require evidence much stronger than simply the unsupported statements that someone else saw a spaceship. On the other hand, a receiver who already believes that teenagers are "capable of anything" is readily able to accept as complete support for the proposition that teenagers are all juvenile delinquents, a similar unsupported statement from a source who states he saw two teenagers steal a car.

The term **evidence** is, in general, used to refer to any attempt to support a proposition. In oral communication, such attempts will normally be found in the statements the speaker makes, although there are occasions when other types of physical evidence, such as charts, diagrams, witnesses, etc., may be used as evidence. The classification scheme we shall use in this volume is one that is applicable both to evidential statements and to other types of evidence.

For the legal profession, evidence has been used to refer to the means by which an alleged matter of fact is established or proved. Such means might include inferences drawn from statements of fact, the testimony of expert witnesses, confessions, and the like. The rules developed by lawyers to determine whether a particular piece of evidence should be admitted for consideration are complicated. They have been refined over a period of centuries and are concerned only with the establishment of the truth of a statement of fact.

A typical speech communicator, however, is concerned not only with the establishment of the truth of statements of fact but also with questions of public policy. He may be interested in deciding whether his community should build a swimming pool, whether a particular political candidate is the better man, or whether the United States should support the government of South Vietnam. These are questions that express an idea about future activities and are clearly different from questions concerned with trying to decide the guilt of an individual on trial for robbery. **Policy questions,** however, depend for their adoption or rejection upon the evidence that can be accumulated through consideration of past events and projections into the future.

Thus the same kinds of evidence are used to support questions of policy as are used to support questions of fact. A closer examination of the category system used by many lawyers to classify the types of evidence they use will further our understanding of the use of evidence in examining both questions of fact and questions of policy.

Types of evidence

It is impossible to categorize evidence in such a way that the categories do not overlap to some extent. Furthermore, the classification scheme we have chosen does not account fully for **all** statements that might be used as proof. Our original definition suggested that any statement might be used as proof by a source and taken as proof by an auditor. Our classification scheme, however, is one that does allow for the analysis and categorization of many of the types of evidence used in speech communication.

Direct evidence is evidence that is immediately and directly related to the question under consideration. Thus, during the trial in an accident case, a witness may state, "I saw the car hit the little girl." This is direct evidence, evidence that represents knowledge gained from use of the senses and that is immediately related to the issue in question.

In considering policy questions, direct evidence might consist in the reporting of some event that was personally witnessed. For example, a driver proceeding over a well-traveled bridge might see the car ahead swerve to miss a hole in the roadbed and hit the retaining wall. His observation might well serve as sufficient evidence to argue that the county commissioner ought to have the roadbed repaired. Another example of the use of direct evidence in questions of public policy might come from a man who was robbed while walking home from the bus through a dark area and who subsequently argues for the installation of street lights. Similarly, a speaker may be convinced that better fire protection is necessary when it takes the fire department twenty-five minutes to get to his burning home. Each of these situations is concerned with the use of evidential materials arrived at through the senses—seeing, hearing, touching, tasting, and smelling —evidence that the communicator believes is directly related to the policy question under consideration.

It should be noted, however, that the situations mentioned above are concerned with evidence that has been obtained by the communicator and then transmitted to a receiver. It is quite likely that an auditor may not see the importance or relevancy of the evidence, nor will most auditors be as concerned with something that happened to the speaker as is the speaker himself. If I am listening to you argue for street lights and have not been robbed, I may be inclined to depreciate your evidence and say that what happened was "an isolated case." Or an auditor might argue that while the evidence is certainly true, it does not support the proposition the speaker says it does. Thus a listener might argue that the fire department is not at fault because it took twenty-five minutes to get to the scene of the fire: the fault lies with the poor access roads leading to the burning house. He might argue that what is needed is not better fire protection but better roads. No listener has argued that the direct evidence supplied in these cases is not accurate, but they have argued that the evidence supplied is not adequate support for the question of policy in which the speaker is interested. The fact that listeners can, and do, question the applicability of direct evidence to questions of policy or questions of fact means that the communicator will have to be sure his evidence is as complete and is applied as relevantly as possible.

In many cases, there are no eyewitness accounts of an event. Yet people may be convinced that the event occurred. They become so convinced because of the presence of **indirect,** or **circumstantial, evidence.** In a legal situation, involving a question of fact, one might have the following report:

> I saw John Smith knocking at Jerry Green's door. When the door opened, Smith rushed into the house and slammed the door behind him. About ten minutes later, I heard a rather loud noise. Right after that, John Smith came running out of the house. He ran to his car and drove away. It looked to me as if he had something in his hand, and I thought it might be a gun, so I called the police.

If the police find that Jerry Green has indeed been shot, observers would probably be inclined to agree there is strong evidence that Smith fired the shot. They cannot be positive, because no one saw the shot fired, but the evidence presented might well tend to convince them that Smith is guilty. This kind of evidence is indirect, or circumstantial, evidence.

Several years ago, a group of teenagers were killed in the early hours of the morning after a graduation party. The incident shocked the entire city. Parents began making speeches to civic clubs, to the Board of Education, and to Parent-Teachers groups, advocating that more direct control be taken at graduation parties by school officials and by the parents themselves. The parents argued that the victims had obtained liquor and that this was the reason for the fatal accident. No one had seen the accident, and there was no one who could testify directly to the fact that the teenagers had been drinking. The evidence linking the accident to drinking was strictly circumstantial. But the evidence, though indirect, was strong enough to convince the school-system officials and parents of other students that better control must be exerted over graduation activities. This is an example of the use of circumstantial evidence to support a statement of public policy.

It should be noted that while the distinction between direct and indirect evidence is an important and useful one, it is frequently difficult to distinguish between them. In fact, almost all evidence may actually be indirect in nature. Even an eyewitness to an event may be in error in reporting his observations, and his observations may actually have only the status of indirect evidence rather than direct evidence.

Just as direct evidence may sometimes be used to support more than one proposition, indirect evidence may also be used. In fact, it is more likely to be used as evidential material to support more than one proposition. In the example we have just cited, it is possible to argue that the teenagers' deaths could be related to the sale of liquor in the city, to the inspection of automobiles for safety, to the necessity for increased police protection, or to the need for raising the driving age for teenagers. In some circumstances, indirect evidence is all that is available to the communicator when he attempts to support a particular policy question. When this is the situation, it should be remembered that the case must normally be made much stronger. This is particularly true when a number of alternative courses of action are available to the auditor. If a speaker decides that a particular course of action is the best available, then he must be sure the weight of the evidence he is using points to the course of action he advocates and not to some other course of action that might be advocated by another communicator.

Direct evidence is linked in a positive manner to a question under consideration. But sometimes it is impossible to find evidence directly linked to a proposition. In such a situation it may be necessary to support a proposition by showing that it is impossible to support its opposite. For example, black leaders argue that there is discrimination in housing in the North because there are no blacks living in white neighborhoods. This is **negative evidence.** Blacks might not be living in certain places for many reasons, but since discrimination is frequently difficult to prove with direct, positive evidence, it is necessary to turn to negative evidence to support the proposition.

Negative evidence is not always admissible in United States courts. Yet we all use negative evidence to conduct much of our daily life. Business institutions use negative evidence in checking on an individual's credit rating. It cannot be proven directly that an individual is a good credit risk. But it can be shown that an individual has never defaulted on payments owed to any agency, and this negative evidence is sufficient to allow a store to grant credit. When the government wants to make a security check on an individual who is applying for a position in a sensitive agency, one piece of evidence is the absence of a police record. If no police record exists, the assumption is made that the individual is honest. When a company wants to hire a new employee, they might go through the same type of check with school officials and the police. Failure to have a police record is almost always equated with being an acceptable candidate.

Clearly, any decisions made as a result of considering negative evidence are open to serious question. Just because a man does not have a police record is no guarantee that he is honest. It may simply be that he has never been caught. The speech communicator must be extremely careful in the use of negative evidence. He must be careful both in his use of such evidence in arriving at his own decisions and in using such evidence in communicating ideas to an audience.

Much of the evidence used in public speaking situations must come from materials gathered by others. Usually the communicator who is trying to decide which side to support on a policy question is not able to view all the evidence for himself. He must turn to the reported experiences of others in order to obtain enough evidence to either support or reject any proposition. Some of that evidence will be available from individuals whose best interest will be served if the policy question is decided in a particular way. The evidence, then, works to their advantage. In other cases, however, evidence might be available from someone whose interests will be served only if the question is decided in a way opposite to that in which the evidence seems to point. These individuals are said to be giving **reluctant evidence.**

In a criminal case, the defendant might take the stand and admit that he was near the scene of the crime at the time when the crime was supposed to have been committed. This would be reluctant evidence, because it clearly would be to the interest of the defendant to be able to show that he was far away from the scene of the crime at the time the crime took place. In matters of public policy, a public official might testify that his department was not run as efficiently as he might hope. Several years ago, a newspaper in a Midwestern city reported that certain food stores were adulterating their hamburger with horse meat and thus making large profits. In the ensuing investigation, the director of the city health department admitted that stores were not inspected very often and that when they were, only a cursory glance was given to the products in them. His testimony, given reluctantly, resulted in stronger laws against adulteration and a complete revamping of the inspection system. Included in the changes was the dismissal of the director of the health department. His reluctant evidence led to drastic changes, including changes in his own future.

Most people are inclined to place considerable weight on evidence coming from a reluctant witness, although the testimony he gives may be no more true than evidence that is not reluctant. But the credibility of the witness seems to most of us to be better established when he is testifying against what seem to be his best interests.

Evidence consisting of things is called **real evidence.** Real evidence includes photographs, movies, X-rays, maps, diagrams, experiments, or physical objects. In deciding a question of fact, a jury may be shown a gun that convinces them that a particular individual was guilty of a crime. Or a picture may be shown that convinces an observer a building was in very poor condition. In law, particularly in jury trials, the introduction of real evidence is extremely important. Such evidence allows the judge and jury to "see for themselves" in a way that cannot be duplicated by written depositions or even by eyewitness accounts.

Real evidence is as important in the discussion of policy questions as in a court trial. However, it is frequently difficult for the communicator to make effective use of real evidence. After all, if he is discussing the necessity of building a new civic center, he cannot actually bring the old civic center into the hall to show his audience that a new building is in order. In some situations, however, physical evidence can be used effectively by the speaker concerned with a policy question. Imagine that the quality of construction of a particular sidewalk by a city crew responsible for laying new sidewalks and curbs has been questioned. The speech communicator might decide for himself whether the sidewalks are in good shape by making a direct inspection of a number of places on the questioned sidewalks. If he does find it to be in poor condition, that will tend to fix his own decision. He must now communicate his decision to an auditor or group of auditors. He might do so with a picture of the sidewalk or with a diagram of the cracks that extended throughout the concrete, or he might bring in a piece of the crumbling concrete and pass it around among his auditors. In each case, the speaker would be making use of real evidence.

In 1962, refugees escaping from Cuba offered evidence that the Russians had begun building missile sites in Cuba. The evidence consisted of eyewitness statements about such construction. This evidence was apparently gathered and evaluated. But it was not until photo-reconnaissance planes brought back pictures of the missile sites under construction that the government took direct action. Eyewitness accounts were important, but the availability of real evidence was decisive.

One caution should be noted in the use of real evidence. It is quite possible to fake evidence. Tape recordings can be edited. Eyewitness films can be edited to show something quite different from what the camera saw. Paintings can and have been faked. The results of experiments can be distorted to show a result that was actually not obtained. In using real evidence, the source must be extremely careful to validate the materials in order to reduce the chances that his evidence has been faked.

When man first developed written languages, he made it possible to create evidence that could be used later to support propositions. Evidence may be created for the specific purpose of being used as evidence. **Created evidence** may be contrasted with **accidental evidence,** materials not prepared to be specifically used as evidence but discovered and then applied as evidence.

Lawyers have used created evidence for centuries. Documents such as wills, notes, mortgages, and contracts are prepared so that evidence will be available if a question ever arises about the problem under consideration. Such created evidence has the advantage that it is in written form and may be checked for accuracy even after the passage of many years. A second advantage is that such evidence may be made specific to a particular question and is thus not so likely to be attributed to some other proposition.

In policy questions, created evidence is frequently used. Indeed, many newsmen have commented on the frequency with which public officials create evidence for later use. A question of public policy arises, and a proponent of the question asks an official to make a statement that he can use in discussion about the policy. For example, anticipating a legislative discussion over school aid, the superintendent of public instruction for the state may release information on the state of school district finances. This material will then be used in the legislative discussion as created evidence to support increased school aid. The superintendent is aware that every year there will be a discussion about school financing, and he creates the evidence he thinks he will need ahead of time.

From the discussion above, it may seem as if we are arguing for the manufacture of spurious information. This is not our intent. Many questions of public policy are known in advance. Every year, the state and national legislatures consider appropriations for many activities. When a new school is built, the community frequently knows far ahead of time that a school will eventually be needed. What is suggested here is that in matters such as these, there will be legislative and feasibility studies designed to study particular questions regarding the proposed policies. If the communicator can make use of such studies in the creation of his messages, he may enhance the chances he has to win belief to his side of the proposition.

It may seem that more reliance should be placed on accidental evidence than on evidence created for a specific purpose. And it is certainly true that evidence can be created in such a way as to falsely indicate support for a proposition. On the other hand, created evidence may tell a more precise story because it was created with a particular question in mind. Accidental evidence, while seeming to bear more weight with the typical auditor, may have been gathered or stated in such a fashion that it may be applied to several questions, not just to the one under consideration.

Each of the types of evidence discussed may be applied to many different kinds of questions. Strictly speaking, it would be most desirable for us to have direct, firsthand knowledge of all the events pertaining to any question of public policy and to be able to show real evidence to our audiences as we attempt to support our propositions. In practice, of course, the average citizen does not have the time or the means to absorb firsthand all the information available on even a minor matter of public policy. For example, suppose that the proposition under consideration is to increase school taxes to pay for more teachers and thus relieve crowded conditions. The average citizen might go to one school in the city and look in a classroom window to see whether it is crowded. If he is really concerned, he might go to several schools and repeat the experiment. But to do so, he must be able to leave his own job during the middle of the day, obtain permission to visit all of the schools, and actually go into the classrooms. For most people, such a program is impossible.

If it is impossible to observe personally all aspects of a situation or of a question, the average person must take the next best course. He must depend on evidence that has been collected and arranged by others. For most questions of public policy, the communicator must evaluate evidence in the same way as do the people he will later communicate with. He will be dependent for information on hearsay materials, on evidence that he has not been able to verify personally. This means that any tests for the adequacy of evidence must also include tests for determining the adequacy of the reporter of the evidence.

Tests of evidence

Any time a piece of evidence is used to support a proposition, the evidence should be tested. It should fit the proposition under consideration, it should be complete, and all conflicting evidence should be accounted for. Some of the tests for determining whether a proposition has or has not been supported will be discussed in Chapter 5. But three kinds of tests may be applied to any statement in order to determine its adequacy as evidence. These are the tests of **relevancy, materiality,** and **competency.**

Many of us, in listening to a speaker, have discovered that he seems to be giving us information that has little or no relationship to the problem under discussion. The author once listened to a speaker in a public meeting who was speaking in favor of a tight evening curfew on teenagers. His evidence for such a curfew was that every afternoon, after the local high school had closed its doors, a "mob of kids" rode past his house in their "hotrods" and made an excessive amount of noise. His evidence was impressive. He was an actual eyewitness to the scenes he described. Unfortunately, the evidence he was presenting had absolutely nothing to do with the question of whether teenagers should be allowed out after 10 P.M. The presence of teenagers in an automobile at 3 in the afternoon is not relevant to the question of a 10 P.M. curfew.

The question of a curfew is a policy matter, but relevancy is just as important when one is considering support for a statement of fact. For example, suppose that we wished to establish that the price of automobiles has increased over the past twenty years. In order to fully establish our point, we might wish to show that the price of an automobile has increased faster than the cost of living has increased. This would give a much better case than mere evidence that a Ford costs $125 more today than it did twenty years ago. In such a case, it would be perfectly appropriate to introduce evidence comparing the current price of a pound of steak, butter, or chicken with the prices of those items twenty years ago. These items of evidence become relevant with the introduction of the relationship between automobile price and cost of living at the two periods of time being considered.

Relevancy may well seem a simple matter. After all, it would be reasonable to assume that any given piece of evidence either is or is not relevant to the question under discussion. However, making a decision about the relevancy of a piece of evidence may be extremely difficult. In the case of the teenage curfew already cited, a number of people in the audience obviously believed that the statements about teenage behavior in the afternoon **were** relevant to teenage behavior at night. Several of the auditors seemed to have made their decision to support the curfew proposal on the basis of their agreement with the statements regarding teenage behavior after school.

It is easy to take an experience one has had and apply it as evidence to a problem. But for many questions of fact and many policy questions, the potential communicator will have difficulty obtaining direct, relevant evidence. The temptation is great to apply irrelevant evidence in an attempt to arrive at a decision about the problem. The speaker must exercise great care to avoid the application of irrelevant materials to the problems he is considering.

On many questions, literally hundreds of small bits of evidence are available. Some of the evidence may seem significant to the question, and some may seem only remotely related. We say that evidence is **material** to a question under consideration when it is significantly related to that question; as the degree of relationship becomes more and more tenuous, we say that the evidence becomes more and more **immaterial.**

The example cited of United States behavior during the Cuban missile crisis of 1962 illustrates the importance of the question of materiality to decision making and subsequent speech communication. For many months, Cuban refugees had issued a steady stream of reports that the Russians were helping the Castro regime build a series of missile sites. But it was not until President John F. Kennedy had clear photographic evidence that he made a final decision to force removal of the missiles in Cuba and communicated his decision to the world. The photographic evidence was considered to be both relevant and material. The reports were certainly relevant, but for the President they did not form a sufficiently clear picture to be considered material.

In legal situations, materiality may be determined in order to avoid the introduction of evidence that might only cloud the main issues in the case. Suppose a man is accused of stealing a crate of oranges. When the case comes to trial, the defendant's attorney might try asking a witness whether he knows what color an apple is. The chances are that this evidence would be considered immaterial. Whether or not the witness knows the color of an orange might be relevant to the case, but the court might decide that apples are not material to the main trial issue. In essence, the court would be saying that there might be a relationship between the evidence presented and the trial issue, but that the evidence is tenuous at best and should not be allowed to cloud the main issue.

In policy questions, materiality is also important. Consider the question of whether a community should build a new civic center. Imagine a speaker suggesting that the new civic center should not be built because, when the new city hall was built, the contractors cheated the city, and the cost to the taxpayers was far more than it was supposed to be. Such evidence, while it might be considered relevant to the decision by some listeners, is clearly not material to the question of whether a new civic center is needed. Materiality and relevancy must be considered together. Evidence that is both relevant and material is significantly stronger than evidence that fails to meet one of these two tests.

In the legal situation, evidence is not considered admissible unless it is declared to be **competent.** To be competent, the evidence must be both adequate and sufficient to establish the point under consideration. For example, a layman would not be allowed to testify concerning the medical cause of death. A witness might testify that he saw Sam shoot Jim, but it would take a physician's testimony to establish that Jim died from gunshot wounds in the chest. Laymen are not allowed to testify as to the legal sanity of a defendant. A photograph that is blurred or that gives evidence of having been tampered with would not be admitted as competent evidence. If it can be established that a prospective witness was under the influence of alcohol or drugs at the time his observations took place, his testimony would probably not be taken seriously. In this and the other situations described, the evidence that is to be produced is not competent.

When moving from questions of fact in the legal situation to a consideration of public policy questions, competency is still important. But some of the grounds on which competency is determined must change. When a speaker concerns himself with policy questions, he is usually concerned with the competency of the **individuals** providing information. Not the evidence alone, but the competency of the individuals providing the evidence concerns him. In other words, he must consider the credibility of the witness.

The concern with individual competency, or credibility, takes two forms. The competency of the individuals supplying evidence to the speaker must be considered. But the credibility of the speaker is equally important to a successful speech. Remember that auditors ask themselves the same questions about a speaker as the speaker asks about the informants from whom he gets information. Thus the same criteria that govern credibility for the sources of evidence also govern the credibility of the speaker himself. A number of these criteria are discussed below in the form of questions that may be asked about a source or a witness.

1. Is the individual in a position to have access to the information? When a speaker declares that a traffic light is needed at a particular

corner because small children have been hit there, his listeners are more likely to place faith in his testimony if he lives close to the corner than if he has never been near it. When the issue is foreign policy toward a particular country, a listener is more inclined to place confidence in someone who has been in the country than in someone who has not. Having access to information is clearly important in establishing the competency of an individual. But we must remember that merely being present does not guarantee accurate information. An old experiment still being run in many college classrooms indicates this. The class is sitting and listening to a lecture when the door opens and a person runs down in front of the stage and fires a gun at the professor. Then he runs out of the room. The professor falls to the floor, then gets up, explains that it was all a joke, and asks the class to write an account of the incident. Even though all the people in the class were watching and saw the incident, each person will report something different. We all tend to see what we expect to see, and this selective perception means that we cannot always depend on being able to accept evidence merely because an individual was apparently in a position to observe an incident. In spite of the cautions that we ought to exercise regarding the testimony of eyewitnesses, credibility is improved when we can produce evidence from individuals who have been in a position to observe a series of events carefully.

2. Is the individual qualified in the area under consideration? If a community is considering the building of a new sewage plant, opposition testimony might be presented on the grounds that "the water tastes all right, so why are we worried about a new sewage system?" If this testimony is opposed by that of the city health director, who testifies that "the new sewage system is needed because our tests show that dangerous bacteria are showing up in the drinking water supplied from the city wells," the residents would probably be inclined to trust the health director's testimony. He will be considered more knowledgeable, more qualified than a layman on this particular question. An expert is particularly important when the acquisition of evidence requires some interpretation. When concerned with public health, one consults officials in that area. Education issues call for expert consultants in education. Even with the best of intentions, an individual who is completely untrained in an area may have difficulty interpreting what he is observing.

3. Is the individual reporting all of the available evidence? It is

extremely easy to select only the evidence that seems to support a particular side. Even when an individual is not being "fooled" into selective perception, he usually finds it difficult to remember everything that occurred. Eyewitnesses tend to remember those portions of an event that seem to fulfill their own expectations; they may not report all the details necessary for a communicator to make up his own mind about some question. In judging the competency of an individual, one must be able to estimate whether or not he is reporting all the available information on the topic. If a speaker makes an estimate and is wrong, it could well mean that he will find himself deciding to support one side of a question when he should have supported the other side.

4. Is the individual personally involved with the issue? By this question, we attempt to isolate those individuals who have a personal stake in the outcome of an event or proposition. If an individual has just had a child killed by a car driven by an old man, he might very well wish to support legislation ordering the retesting of all drivers over sixty-five years of age. In fact, such an individual might offer his personal testimony in support of such a proposition. If we stopped our search for evidence at this point, we might well agree with the witness. If we seek further information, however, we might find that this was the only such case in the state that year and that setting up such testing machinery for what is an isolated incident is not justified. We know that it is not possible to secure all testimony from neutral observers, nor is it possible for us to be completely neutral when we speak to an audience. However, the appearance of objectivity is important to listeners, and whether we are giving a speech or seeking information to support a proposition, more faith can be placed in the individual who does not seem to be personally profiting from the testimony he gives.

Each of the questions above is designed to help the communicator establish the competency of the evidence he is evaluating. If the communicator is not able to "see for himself," then he must establish the competency of the sources on which he is relying. After he makes such a determination regarding the competency of these sources of evidence and makes a decision regarding the relation of that evidence to the propositions he is considering, he must also realize that he too will be judged by his auditors in the same manner as that in which he judges his original informants.

Presenting evidence

Our concentration in the first two parts of this chapter has been on the collection of evidence and the testing of that evidence for its relationship to the proposition and the audience. The speech communicator, however, is still faced with the problem of preparing a message in such a way that the audience will understand the testimony or the data he has so laboriously collected. In many cases, evidence is presented so poorly that the auditor simply does not understand either the evidence or the way in which it is related to the proposition under consideration. Complicated economic data, for example, are not easily understood when the communicator merely "talks his way through them." If the same data had been placed in graph or chart form, however, the auditor might more easily grasp the speaker's intent.

This section will concentrate on the presentation of data in visual forms. The speech communicator normally is qualified to organize his thoughts and evidence for an oral presentation of the material. What is forgotten, however, is the fact that many kinds of evidence are better presented in a visual form, accompanied by an oral explanation, than in an oral form alone. Two general principles may guide a speaker when deciding to utilize a particular visual presentation. First, he should turn to some type of visual presentation when time and space demands such a presentation. When the evidence is complicated, when presentation in an oral fashion would require significant amounts of time, when the evidence consists of statistical information, or when complicated operations are involved, some type of visual presentation is almost always justified. Second, he should use visual materials to secure attention to the evidence he has to present. A verbal description of a robbery attempt will not have the impact on an audience that a series of snapshots made of the robbers leaving the scene of the crime will have.

Many types of visual presentation are possible. The speech communicator should take advantage of a blackboard or flip chart, at the very least, to diagram some of the pieces of evidence he wishes to present. He may introduce actual models to the situation or even have the audience members handle a piece of the evidence. In jury trials, the prosecutor will always try to have each member of the jury handle the "murder weapon" for the effect such handling has on the jury members. Charts showing the organization of a company, a diagram of a house, and the traditional "pie" diagram to show the disposition of state and local taxes are extremely useful in presenting evidence visually to an audience. The use of maps, graphs, or pictures may also serve to make evidence more striking and telling to an audience.

A few words of caution ought to be mentioned about the use of visual aids. Most of us have been in the situation where the speaker tried to illustrate a point with a visual aid so small that we could not see it from where we were sitting. Such evidence is worse than presenting the material orally. **Size** is a criterion variable in presenting visual evidence. Whatever is used must be used in such a way that everyone in the group can see it easily and clearly. Visual presentations ought to include only those **details** that are essential to the point being made. Use of a photograph cluttered with people to illustrate the beauty of a building in the background is an example of visual aid that will merely detract from the point being made. Visual materials must be **neat** in appearance. An audience member must be able to look at the material and immediately see the relationship between the evidence being presented and the proposition under discussion. Sloppy art work, blurred photographs, cluttered diagrams all detract from the desired impression.

In the next chapter, we shall discuss some of the more important ways of laying out evidential material so that an auditor will see its relationship to a proposition. But we must remember that no matter how logically we plan our evidence, if the audience does not understand what we are saying, our efforts to secure belief changes will be in vain—thus the importance of good visual materials to speech communication.

Summary

This chapter has been concerned with evidence. Evidence lies all around us. No matter what the question is—a matter of fact or a question of policy—the speech communicator must depend on evidence in order to make up his own mind and to be successful in communicating his ideas. The communicator may choose from several types of evidence: direct, indirect, negative, reluctant, real, or created. The type of evidence available depends on the relation of the communicator to the necessary evidence. The communicator may have to depend entirely on evidence produced by others if the topic concerns foreign policy, whereas he himself may have direct knowledge of his community's needs.

Once a source of evidence is found, it must be judged for the adequacy and completeness of the evidence it makes available. The criteria used in this evaluation are the three grounds of relevancy, materiality, and competency. When judging evidence, the communicator should keep in mind that there are two aspects of evidence. He must judge the adequacy of the available evidence in order to make accurate decisions on his own, and he must also be concerned with the way in which any available evidence is likely to appear to an audience.

Finally, the speech communicator must be concerned with the actual presentation to his listeners of the evidence he has accumulated. Extremely complicated evidence cannot be presented orally with the same effectiveness as it can be presented visually. The communicator must examine his evidence closely in order to determine the most effective method of presenting it.

FIVE

Modes of proof: inference

A single piece of evidence may establish the truth or falsity of a proposition. An eyewitness account of a shooting may be the only evidence needed to convict an individual of murder. A single accident at a dangerous intersection may be sufficient to mobilize community action. A school fire may lead to changes in the fire regulations for an entire state. Each of these is a situation in which a single piece of evidence was used in a communication situation to support another proposition. The more usual situation, however, is that in which the communicator is faced by many pieces of data and has to arrive at a conclusion consistent with all of them.

In order to draw conclusions successfully, to explain those conclusions to others, or to predict a series of future events, the communicator must make use of the **inferential process.** He must take the evidence he has accumulated, place the evidence into some structural arrangement, and attempt to determine exactly what propositions may be inferred from the evidence. Whether the intent of the source is to attempt to prove the truth of a statement of fact or to concern himself with a policy statement, the inferential process must be used to establish any proposition. Over the centuries men have developed several **modes of proof,** i.e., kinds of structural arrangements that may be used to establish the essential truth or falsity of a proposition.

Before examining some of these structural arrangements in detail, it is interesting to note just how important inferences are to the speech communicator. Each of the following statements represents one type of inference, that is, a **prediction: a statement made about what will occur or should occur in the future:**

1. It will rain in Michigan tomorrow.
2. The President will be reelected for a second full term.
3. The United Nations will live to celebrate its fortieth birthday.
4. There will be a Third World War within the next five years.
5. Man will land on the planet Mars before 1980.

Each of these statements is an inference. None of them is capable of immediate verification, although eventually all of them may be verified as either true or false. None of the statements was made "off the top of the head"; there is solid data that may be used to substantiate each of them. Spend a few minutes thinking back over the last week and try to remember the number of times you used an inference in speaking to someone or heard an inference made by another speaker. It is possible that you either made or listened to at least one statement asserting something about the future in almost every extended conversation.

Statements about the future are only one kind of inference. Another important kind of inference is the **generalization: a statement that draws together a number of observations.** The following are examples of inferences that generalize:

1. College students at Michigan State University come from the top quarter of their high-school graduating class.
2. The United States always wins the wars it enters.
3. Women have a longer life span than men.
4. Most Americans do not attend church regularly.
5. Children who are good readers have more access to books than do poor readers.

A generalization takes individual pieces of evidence and attempts to draw a conclusion that is representative of the entire set of statements. One would decide that the inference about winning wars is correct if he looked into history, determined the number of times the United States engaged in war, and counted the number of times the United States won the war. If he finds that the United States won every war it entered, then he would be entitled to make the generalization, "The United States always wins the wars it enters."

A third type of inference is the **explanation: a statement that points to the cause for an event or series of events.** Frequently, such inferences are phrased as a question, but the intent of the question is clearly inferential, because the author is usually interested in the "why" or the "because" of a statement. Such questions include:

1. Why did North Korea attack South Korea?
2. What causes icebergs?
3. What is the relationship between gun ownership and suicide?
4. What causes cancer?
5. Why does the United States have a high unemployment rate?

As they are phrased, the questions are not inferences. But each implies an inference. When one asks, "Why did North Korea attack South Korea?" the suggestion is that there is a set of statements that, when examined, will provide a statement answering the question. Such a statement will be in the form of an inference. In this case, depending on the evidence available, answers to the original question might include: "The Russians ordered North Korea to attack South Korea," "North Korea wanted more territory," or "North Korea wanted to reunite the country under Communist rule." All these statements are inferences and, taken together, constitute an explanation. Explanations usually differ in nature from the set of statements one might use to predict that another world war will break out within five years. Normally, explanations involve a search for causes of events, or for the relationships between events. Like other kinds of inferences, explanations attempt to interpret the world in ways that make it easier to grasp that world.

Patterns of inference

Predictions, generalizations, and explanations represent situations in which man has attempted to arrange sets of sentences into patterns that will allow him to derive conclusions that will be agreed to by others. Some of the patterns developed to enable us to derive inferences are very old. The Greek philosophers talked about the classical syllogism, and it is a pattern still used today. Other patterns are newer or have been developed from earlier models.

Patterns of inference are examined with two main criteria in mind.

We try to develop **rigorous** patterns, i.e., patterns of analysis that are precise and strict in their rules for examination of the statements comprising the pattern. We also attempt to develop **reliable** patterns. Reliability is expressed in two ways: (1) the ability to apply the same pattern to any similar set of data with the same result and (2) the ability to have different individuals use the same pattern and obtain the same results.

The speech communicator is looking for inferential patterns he may apply in that portion of his speech preparation in which he is looking for conclusions about which he may be confident. If he finds the patterns, he may use them in building a speech about his conclusions. However, the complexity required of some patterns of inference may preclude his inclusion of the entire pattern in the actual speech. The question of building the most persuasive structural pattern for actual speech presentation will be considered in Chapter 7. The present chapter's concern is with an analysis of the inferential process.

The following discussion will examine five different patterns, or structures, commonly used to derive inferences. Some evidence indicates that these four patterns are not completely independent, that there are points of overlap, but each pattern seems complete enough to consider separately. They are: (1) the deductive pattern, (2) the Toulmin pattern, (3) the probabilistic pattern, (4) the functional pattern, and (5) the genetic pattern.

The deductive pattern

The oldest of all forms of logic, the deductive pattern, was first described in detail by Aristotle in his two works, **Prior Analytics** and **Posterior Analytics.** The pattern was considered the most acceptable model for scientists until the Middle Ages. It has been supplanted by other inferential-process models today, but it is still an extremely useful model for the analysis of the inferences drawn from various types of evidence. The simplest of all deductive forms is the **classical syllogism,** which can serve as a model to illustrate deduction and some of the strengths and weaknesses associated with this inferential form.

Most people have run across the most famous syllogism:

> All men are mortal.
> Socrates was a man.
> Therefore, Socrates was mortal.

What does this pattern contain? In logical terms, it first contains a very general premise: "All men are mortal" with two terms, "men" and "mortal." Then it contains a premise that relates a third term "Socrates" to the first term: "Socrates is a member of the class of men." And finally, it contains a conclusion, and inference, linking the second term to the third term: "Socrates is then related to the class of mortals." If we look at the same syllogism in terms of evidence, we would suggest that the first two statements in the pattern are evidential statements, while the third statement is the inference to be drawn from a consideration of the two pieces of evidence. This is the pattern for all deductions, no matter how complicated they become. Some evidence or premises are stated, and conclusions or inferences are then made from the premises.

Before proceeding further, the concept of **validity** must be introduced and defined. The communicator who is concerned with the development of patterns, or models, wants to be able to use those models in many different situations with many different types of data. Such patterns should be independent of the physical world, should be patterns that would make it possible to reliably draw inferences from mathematical concepts or nonsense syllables if desired. When a pattern is internally consistent and its parts "hang together," the argument is considered **valid.** Validity and the truth that comes from verification are independent of each other. A conclusion may be false, yet be derived from an argument that is valid. Consider the following argument:

All students are women.
All women are basketball players.
Therefore, all students are basketball players.

The conclusion is obviously false, but the pattern is valid. It is internally consistent. Why should anyone be concerned with developing a tool that will enable him to make inferences that might be false? The answer lies in the relationship between verification and validity. **If** one has a valid argument, and **if** one tests his two premises and finds that they are true, then he can be positive that the conclusion is also true, without the further need for verification of the truth of the conclusion. The power of deduction lies in this fact. It enables us to derive new statements about the world from statements that have already been tested. We **know** that the derived inferences are true if the logical structure used was adequate. Thus the test for the deductive pattern is whether or not it is a valid pattern.

When Aristotle developed and amplified the ideas that Greek philosophers had about the syllogism, he did so on the basis of four general types of sentences or statements. These are:

Type	Structure	Example
A	All A is B.	All Russians are Communists.
E	No A is B.	No Swedes are citizens of Japan.
I	Some A is B.	Some Americans are students.
O	Some A is not B.	Some women are not students.

The A and E sentence types are called **universals,** whereas the I and O types are referred to as **particulars.** The sentence types obviously fit many different situations, and any word representing an individual or a class of objects may be placed where A and B occur in them.

To form an argument that may be analyzed according to that deductive pattern represented by the syllogism, one merely states his argument in the form suggested by the sentence types. The classical syllogism has three such sentences, such as AAA, EIO, or AIO. Then one must examine the resulting structure to determine whether the last sentence in the structure, the conclusion, has been validly derived. To make this examination, one needs a set of rules. Over the years, logicians have developed several such sets of rules. Each of them differs only slightly from the others, although some of the differences may make a difference in the way a pattern is analyzed, as we shall see. The set we shall use for illustration of the process of deduction is that developed by Ambrose and Lazerowitz.[1]

Before presenting a set of rules for determining the validity of a syllogism, the term **distribution** must be defined. Look at the A sentence type. Ask yourself whether you have looked at all the members of the class being discussed or only at a portion of that class. In the sentence "All Russians are Communists," you have had to look at "All Russians" in order to make the statement that they are "all Communists." On the other hand, you do not have to look at all the Communists to make the statement. There might be many other members of the class Communist than those who are Russians. The term **Com-**

[1] Alice Ambrose and Morris Lazerowitz, **Fundamentals of Symbolic Logic** (New York: Rinehart, 1948), pp. 255–277.

munist is **not distributed.** In the E sentence type, both A and B are distributed. When one says, "No Swedes are citizens of Japan," he must have looked at all "Swedes" and all "citizens of Japan." So both terms are distributed. In the I type, neither term is distributed. In the O type, the B term is distributed, but the A term is not.

A second word that must be defined is the **middle term.** Look at the arrangement:

All A is B. (Major Premise)
All B is C. (Minor Premise)
Therefore, all A is C. (Conclusion)

Here the term B appears in both of the first two premises. This is called the **middle term.** If there is no middle term, there is no syllogism, and nothing can be logically inferred from the arrangement. Another way of looking at the problem is to understand that the middle term is the term that appears in both premises but drops out in the conclusion. Thus a syllogism consists of three and only three terms laid out in two premises and a conclusion. There are, of course, many other logical forms, but the classical syllogism is best used for our purposes of illustrating the nature of logical proof.

If one has a set of three sentences containing only three terms, and each sentence is of the A, E, I, or O type, one can determine the **validity of the conclusion** produced by applying the following rules to the pattern:

1. The middle term must be distributed in at least one of the sentences.

2. No term undistributed in the premises may be distributed in the conclusion.

3. If either of the first two premises are of the A or E type, the conclusion must be of the A or E type.

4. If both premises are negative, no conclusion can be drawn.

5. If one premise is negative, then the conclusion must also be negative.

6. If neither premise is negative, the conclusion must be positive.

7. If both premises are particular (either I or O types), no conclusion can be drawn.

8. If the major premise is I and the minor premise is negative, no conclusion can be drawn.

This is the formal set of rules that may be applied to any syllogism in order to determine whether or not it is valid. We should again note that we have chosen only one possible set of rules. The Ambrose and Lazerowitz rules are those favored by most modern logicians, but they would not necessarily be favored by all logicians. In particular, rule 3 is the denial of an existential assumption in A and E type propositions. Aristotle did not deny such an assumption and consequently accepted some forms as valid which the use of our rules would deny.

Let us look at some examples and apply the rules to see if the syllogisms are valid.

1. All A is B.
   All C is B.
   Therefore, all C is A.

This syllogism is invalid. Rule 1 applies, because the middle term, B, is not distributed in either premise.

2. All A is B.
   No C is A.
   Therefore, no C is B.

This syllogism is invalid. Rule 2 applies, because the B term is not distributed in the first premise but is distributed in the conclusion.

3. Some A is B.
   All B is C.
   Therefore, some A is C.

This syllogism is valid. A check with the rules indicates that no violation has occurred.

4. No A is B.
   All A is C.
   Therefore, some C is not B.

This syllogism is invalid. Rule 3 applies, because we have a particular conclusion with universal premises. Note that this is the case mentioned above where Aristotle would have ruled this syllogism as valid, because his set of rules does not deny an existential assumption in A and E propositions.

The syllogism seems to be a powerful tool for the analysis of arguments and the examination of data. The **real value of the syllogism** lies in its ability to analyze relationships between statements. If one has two premises (or two pieces of evidence) that he has examined in some way and knows to be true, he can make a syllogism in which the conclusion will also be a true statement related to the two premises. There is no need to test the truth of the conclusion, since correctness of the pattern assures the truth of a conclusion following validly from evidence that is true.

The reader might well wonder why, if this is such a powerful tool, it is not used as the basis for all science as well as for all communication? Although powerful, syllogistic logic has serious limitations. For one thing, the classical syllogism is limited to expressions falling within one of the four sentence types we have discussed. Relatively few sentences found in ordinary discourse actually are of one of these types, although many could perhaps be translated into one. A second serious limitation is that complicated situations are difficult to analyze using syllogistic logic. For example, consider the following argument:

> The United States must always retaliate when its economic and political interests have been crossed. We know this because all countries that have failed to retaliate in such circumstances have eventually been overrun.

This argument may be restated in syllogistic form, although it is more easily cast into two syllogisms. To do so, the logician has to decide what the terms are in the argument. Then he has to decide what the premises are and how they ought to be arranged. When this is done, he is in a position to check the syllogism to see whether it is valid.

Try your hand at putting the above argument into syllogistic form and checking it to see whether or not it is valid. It takes time and is a difficult task. An average listener could not translate such an argument into formal syllogistic style while he was trying to concentrate on the remainder of the speech. If we were to present a more complicated argument, even a highly trained logician would have trouble putting the argument into syllogistic form.

A third serious limitation to the syllogism lies in the difficulty of establishing the truth of the premises. The speech communicator, as well as the auditor, is not only interested in validity but in whether the truth of the conclusion can be established. In our discussion of the syllogism, we have emphasized that it is **only** when the two premises are true and the syllogism is valid that the conclusion is also true. This means that the truth of the premises must be established beyond the shadow of a doubt. In the statement, "All men are mortal," this means we must examine all men in order to ascertain that each and every man we look at is mortal. This is clearly an impossible task; yet if we fail to look at all cases, we cannot establish the conclusion as being true. It is this third restriction that, more than anything else, makes the classical syllogism of relatively little use in communication, and even of limited use in modern science.

To avoid the problems seemingly inherent in the classical syllogism, philosophers have developed other deductive systems. Although there is not enough space to present even some of these models in detail, they should at least be given brief description. The most general way of describing them is to say that they are **propositional calculi.** Such advanced logical systems allow for the development of ways of handling entire propositions containing such terms as "or," "and," "if———, then———," and "if——— and only if———, then———." The logician working with such propositions uses a **truth table** to determine the conditions under which an entire proposition will be either true or false. For example, consider the sentence, "The United States will have wage controls or it will have rationing." This sentence breaks into the form "A or B." Under what conditions is the entire sentence going to be true? We may use a truth table like the one below to determine the conditions:

A	or	B
T	F	T
T	T	F
F	T	T
F	F	F

This table suggests that the entire statement will be true under the condition that one of the two parts of the statement be true and one be false. The logician working with the propositional calculus uses such truth tables to determine the conditions under which quite complicated arguments will be either true or false. The classical syllogism was developed for working with **classes of objects.** The propositional calculus was developed to work with **sets of propositions.**

Whether the communicator uses the syllogism or one of the newer deductive models, his objectives are the same. He is interested in taking statements that have been accepted as evidence and seeing what other statements can be derived from them. The use of deduction in the analysis of speech materials should not be confused with the presentation of materials in oral communication. In the actual presentation, the communicator may well choose to eliminate mention of certain obvious premises, to state the conclusion without any premises at all, or to reword the conclusion so that it will make better semantic sense to the auditor. In fact, the auditor may never know from the manner in which the speech is presented that the conclusion actually was arrived at as the result of a deductive analysis.

In the speech itself, one expects to find such statements as "Democracy is the best system of government for the United States," "All juvenile delinquents ought to be taught how to behave by placing them in jail," "John Doe will be arrested soon, because he has been placed on the FBI's Most Wanted List," or "The typhoid breakout means that our community needs a new sewage system." These and similar statements represent truncated syllogisms, syllogisms with one premise omitted, or syllogisms in which parts of premises have been stated but not the entire argument. For example, one of the statements above may be put into full syllogistic form as:

> All persons on the FBI's Most Wanted List are persons who will
> probably be arrested soon.
> John Doe is a person on the FBI's Most Wanted List.
> John Doe is a person who will probably be arrested soon.

The technical term for an argument that appears in this shortened version is **enthymeme**. Enthymemes represent one of the most important sources of speech materials. They have a deductive pattern in back of the statement as it is heard by the listener, and the speech communicator ought to be able to make a deductive analysis for his own information and also for auditors who might question the statement without such an analysis.

Deduction is a powerful tool. With it, a communicator may derive conclusions from evidential materials. With it, he may determine the validity of many linguistic structures that he might be using. With it, he may establish the truth of statements without the necessity of making observations himself. It is one of the major ways in which the communicator may establish proof for an audience.

The Toulmin pattern

The deductive pattern, although useful to the speech communicator, has a number of problems severely limiting that usefulness. In order to overcome some of these problems, Stephen Toulmin proposes an alternative way of analyzing data. In his book, **The Uses of Argument,**[2] he suggests that all conclusions—all statements that express a policy based on the consideration of evidential materials—may be stated as a series of propositions relating the evidential materials to the conclusion. In Chapter 7, we shall show how the Toulmin model may actually be used to organize and present complicated speech ma· terials. Here, we present the basic Toulmin approach as an aid in analyzing arguments.

Figure 2 shows the six elements that can be found in any compli-cated argument. Three of these, the **evidence,** the **warrant,** and the

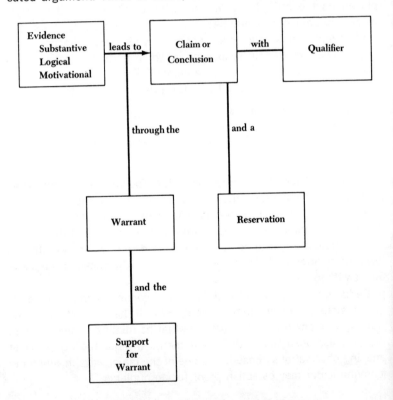

Figure 2. An Adaptation of the Toulmin Model

[2] Stephen Toulmin, **The Uses of Argument** (Cambridge, England: Cambridge University Press, 1958).

claim, are found in all arguments. More complex arguments also include the **qualifier, reservation,** and **support for the warrant.** With these
six elements, Toulmin claims to be able to analyze any argument so
that the relation between the initial data and the final conclusion
becomes clear. Let us take up the six elements and define them in
detail:

1. In its broadest sense, **evidence** is any data that may be used to
establish a conclusion. Any of the types of evidence mentioned in the
previous chapter may be utilized in the Toulmin formulation. Evidence
is used as the basis from which conclusions are drawn. A unit of
evidence may consist in a single proposition representing an observation made by a single individual, or it may be composed of a series of
statements. Evidence may be statistical materials, case histories,
judgments made by an authority, or any other statements from which
people might be inclined to reason.

2. The **claim** is the proposition or conclusion that must follow from
the data. It is the proposition, whether factual, inferential, or judgmental, in which the communicator wishes to induce belief. The
speaker who says, "Unemployment is increasing in the United States,
and the government ought to do something about it," makes use of
an evidential statement in the first clause of the statement to arrive
at a claim in the second clause. The claim may be as simple as the
example we have used, or it may be as complex a series of conclusions
as the late President Kennedy made in his speech to the nation after
reviewing the evidence on the penetration of Soviet missiles into
Cuba.

3. The **warrant** is the statement showing the reasoning that must
have gone on between finding the evidence and making the claim. It
may show the assumptions on which the claim is based or the method
by which the evidence was evaluated. For example, the speaker might
argue, "Unemployment is increasing in the United States, and the
government ought to do something about it, since the state governments have not been able to cope with the problem and the federal
government is obligated to step in when states have been unsuccessful." Here, the last part of the statement is the warrant and indicates
the basis on which the speaker makes his claim.

4. At times, use of the warrant alone provides insufficient justifica-
tion for the claim. When this situation arises, the warrant itself will
need more support in order to justify its use. Such backing is provided

by the **support for the warrant.** For example, in the following argument, the support for the warrant takes the form of an argument from history: "Negro citizens are segregated into ghetto areas in the United States. Therefore, the United States needs a Fair Housing Law, since every citizen ought to be treated equally and history shows that nations who do not provide for equal treatment cannot grow either economically or morally." The last portion of the argument is the support for the warrant.

5. In policy questions, claims may need to be limited in some way. It may be that a claim will be justified if certain conditions are met but not in other circumstances. The **reservation** sets forth the nature of any limitation the communicator wishes to place on the claim he makes. The use of a reservation is seen in the following argument:

> The underdeveloped nations of the world have a more rapidly rising birthrate than the developed nations (**evidence**). The United States should provide these nations with birth-control information that will let them control their population growth (**claim**). We must take this action because we have a moral obligation to help underdeveloped nations (**warrant**). However, we cannot supply such information to nations whose religious or moral principles would outlaw control of births (**reservation**).

Most claims made in policy questions need the addition of a reservation, because there will normally be a hierarchy of policies that could be adopted. Reservations may specify the amount of money that may be used, the future situations that might make the claim unworkable, or the limitations that might be placed on the claim by other policy decisions.

6. The **qualifier** is normally an adjective placed within the statement that forms the claim. To use an old example, take the claim, "Socrates was mortal." If one placed a qualifier within that claim, he would have, "Socrates was probably mortal." The qualifier is a word like "maybe," "mostly," "possibly," or "seldom." It may also be a phrase like "most of the time," "75 percent of the cases," "in fewer than ten," or "only in rare circumstances." The qualifier is important to the communicator in making his decision regarding some claim. A claim that might not be acceptable without qualification could become acceptable with the proper qualifier added to the claim.

These six elements form the basis for the method of analysis proposed by Toulmin as an addition to, or an alternative for, more traditional deductive or inductive methods of analysis. The Toulmin system has the advantage of being an extremely flexible system. It may be applied to many different types of argument and used to analyze either deductive or inductive arguments. It may be used by the layman as a way of quickly assessing the merit of the arguments he hears or reads and also by the communicator in designing a message.

The Toulmin system lacks, however, a clearly stated, rigorous method of testing the completeness of an argument. Even if an argument is presented clearly, there are no rules for determining precisely when a conclusion is fully justified, when enough evidence has been presented, when there is enough support for the warrant, or when the claim follows validly from the evidence. To make such determinations with rigor, the communicator will have to utilize one of the other methods of analysis presented in this chapter.

The Toulmin method of analysis, even with its deficiencies, is perhaps the easiest pattern for the average communicator to utilize. It does not require the logical rigor of the syllogism or the mathematical knowledge of the probabilistic pattern. It may be used with little training. And, as we will see in the final chapter of this book, it may also serve as a method of organizing speech materials for effective presentation.

The probabilistic pattern

In our discussion of the classical syllogism, we mentioned that one of the major limitations of the syllogism was the necessity of determining the truth of the premises. The communicator must be absolutely sure that the premises of the deductive argument are true, or he can say nothing about the truth of the conclusion. When a statement such as "All doctors are competent" is used in an argument, it means that the statement is completely, 100 percent true. It means that the competence of every existing doctor has been determined. This is an obvious impossibility. The best any person could be expected to say is that the statement is **probably true** or **probably false.** The **probabilistic pattern** has been developed in order to examine the large class of statements that may be established as either true or false at a level of certainty less than 100 percent.

At a very simple level, the probabilistic model is easy to examine. Imagine a group of forty people who belong to a club. Every year the club elects a new president. An investigator would like to find out ahead of time who the new president is likely to be. He goes to each member of the club and asks each member for whom he will vote. If he finds out that twenty-four of the forty people intend to vote for Jones, he will conclude that Jones will be the next president of the club. Note that his conclusion, while stated as a fact, is only **probably** true. It could be that some people will change their minds before the vote actually takes place. It is possible that some people deliberately gave false answers to throw him off the track. It is possible that the investigator did not count correctly. It is possible that Jones would not accept the presidency. Other reasons might well intervene to make what was accepted as true turn out to be not true.

The club example is easy because everyone in the group can be asked for his opinion. But let us imagine that one wishes to know who will be the next governor of Michigan. The state has approximately 4,000,000 residents who will be eligible to vote in the next election. One can never ask each and every one of those people for whom he will vote. An investigator may say, "Well, with that many people, I won't need to ask them all. I'll just ask everyone that I can what candidate he will vote for." Suppose that the investigator asks as many as 50,000 of the 4,000,000 eligible voters. Suppose that 55 percent say that they intend to vote for Jack Green. Is 55 percent the same figure which would be obtained if all 4,000,000 were questioned? If the investigator had picked a different 50,000 people, would the percent remain the same? Will all the people asked actually vote on election day? Do the 50,000 people asked come from all areas of the state, or did the investigator concentrate his efforts in the Detroit area? Is there **any** way to be sure that the 55 percent will not be 49 percent on election day?

These are probability questions, questions that ask how a limited number of cases may be examined and yield a statement that will be accurate about a much larger group of people or objects or events. Predictions about election results are only one type of probability question. A probability model must be used if one is interested in whether Russia will be willing to adhere to the terms of a new treaty, in how wide a highway must be for an anticipated load of cars ten years from the completion of construction, in the number of class-rooms needed for a projected elementary school, or in whether a new safety feature for an automobile will save enough lives to justify its cost. Probability questions may be inferences about factual data or may be applied in policy areas. What are the characteristics of questions that must be answered by applying a probability model to the data?

First, the question must be one that attempts to draw some general conclusion from the examination of smaller bits of data. Suppose one wants to establish that juvenile delinquents come from poor home environments. This is the general conclusion to be established. To establish it, one would have to look at the home environments of a good many individual juvenile delinquents. If one found that every juvenile delinquent one looked at had a poor home environment, one would state the conclusion, "Juvenile delinquents have poor home environments." Here one would be going from the specific to the general; this is one major characteristic of probability questions, or as they are sometimes called, **problems in induction.**

Second, the question must be one in which it is impossible to look at all cases. If one asks how many black marbles are in a set of twenty marbles lying on the table, one does not need to state his answer in probability terms. We would just count and report how many there are. But if there is a large jar filled with a mixture of black and white marbles, and someone hands us a handful of the marbles from the jar and wants to know how many black marbles are in the entire jar, we have a probability problem. We must estimate on the basis of the sample drawn from the jar exactly how many black marbles are in the jar. Or, referring to the example of juvenile delinquents mentioned earlier, it is very unlikely that **all** juvenile delinquents can be examined. So the investigator has to estimate the home environment of juvenile delinquents from the sample of delinquents he chooses to look at.

This second requirement needs further explication. When the communicator or scientist or analyst is faced with only a limited number of observations, with some study that he can conduct only once, or with an event that only a few people can observe, general conclusions may be reached only in the form of a "bet" about what the real, true-world situation is. Given this kind of evidence, the communicator is always unsure concerning the correctness of any conclusion he makes about the true state of affairs. The probability model provides ways in which to assess this uncertainty and to calculate the probability that one will be wrong if he makes a given inference. When you have some idea of how wrong you are likely to be in a given situation, you are in a much better position to decide what you can say and do about the situation. For example, if you look at a sample of juvenile delinquents and find that 60 percent come from poor environments, you may conclude that improvement of that environment will lead to a decrease in the number of juvenile delinquents. You could be wrong in analyzing the situation, but at least you will be operating on evidence that establishes the probable truth of the inference.

The third requirement for the application of a probability model to an inferential question is that the events concerned must be of such a nature that they can be **described.** This may seem to be a peculiar requirement, but it becomes less so when one realizes that the model to be built will be largely dependent on an underlying mathematical model. Such a mathematical model demands that the events to be quantified, or numbered, can be separated from other events that differ in any way. If there is absolutely no way of distinguishing between different events, no one will ever be able to draw inferences about the possibility of future occurrences of the events or about the possibility that these events differ from other events.

The final requirement is that the events deal with the **repeatable.** Inferences cannot be drawn about an event unique in time and space. Certainly every event or object or person is unique in some respect, but this requirement suggests only that the events used be repeatable in principle. For example, if I throw a die on the table and obtain a six, it is true that I cannot ever throw that same die in the same way and at the same time. Time passes on, and one can never return to exactly the same spot in space or time. But the probability requirement is merely that I be able to throw the die again. This I can do; thus the event is repeatable.

Let us now assume that a given question has data that fit all the requirements. **The probability that any event will occur may be defined as the proportion of the time that it will happen in the long run.** This definition of probability needs further explication. Assume that one is interested in determining whether or not some observation is really representative of the true state of affairs. How does one decide that it was not just a random, chance happening but is the most likely thing to happen in similar circumstances? For example, if I were to shuffle a deck of cards and ask you to draw a card, and you drew the deuce of hearts, would you then decide that you would draw the deuce of hearts every time I asked you to perform the same task? Most would not make this decision nor bet **any** money at even odds on drawing the same card twice in succession. If the deck is an honest deck and the dealer shuffles the cards honestly, the probability of any one of the fifty-two cards in the deck turning up on a single draw is 1/52. These are small odds. But the probability that the deuce of hearts would be drawn twice in a row is 1/52 times 1/52 or a probability of 1/2704. This possibility is so remote that few would bet on its happening. By chance alone, however, it could happen once in every 2704 times the experiment is repeated.

How does one decide whether or not an inference may be made at a high enough probability level to accord the inference the status of proof? The easiest answer is that it cannot, that these decisions may never be made with absolute certainty and may thus never be said to be in a position to be used as proof. Harder to understand, but perhaps more helpful to the communicator, is the answer that although one may never be absolutely, 100 percent sure that his inferences are going to be correct, he can establish an area of agreement such that any inference established within it is one to be believed in and operated on. The scientist has established several such areas. If he can say that the probability of an event occurring by chance is less than 1/20 or less than 1/100, he will usually say that he is willing to accept the inference as correct. Note, however, that he could be wrong. If an event could occur by chance alone 1 out of 100 times, it might be that the occurrence the investigator selected was that one time. Such an occurrence would be a rare event, but such rare events may cause scientists to say that a statement is true when it is not or to deny the truth of a statement that should be accepted.

Let us look at the process. Imagine a researcher wishes to determine whether a seven-year-old boy is more attracted to a baseball glove than to a doll. The probability pattern says that his first step is to deny that there is **any** relationship between the boy and the baseball glove or between the boy and the doll. In other words, he must hypothesize that the boy will choose equally between the glove and the doll when he is given an equal opportunity to choose either one. Such an hypothesis is called a **null hypothesis** and represents the scientist's initial guess that there is no relationship between the events he is concerned with, i.e., that the boy will choose the baseball glove as many times as he chooses the doll.

Now the researcher sets up an experimental situation. He places the glove and the doll in cabinets and tells the boy to go to a cabinet and choose either the glove or the doll. Imagine that the boy picks the glove. If either event is as likely to occur as the other, the probability of his choosing the glove is 1/2. No one would conclude from this evidence that the null hypothesis should be rejected, because it could be argued that not enough cases have been examined. It might well be that on the very next trial the boy would choose the doll. Therefore, the experimenter does not stop with a single trial. Let us imagine that he has the boy choose three separate times, and each time the boy picks the glove. Now can the experimenter conclude by saying that he has proved that this seven-year-old boy will choose the baseball glove over the doll? To make this decision, he first needs to enumerate what outcomes are possible. If he uses G for a choice of the glove and D for the choice of the doll, there are eight possible arrangements of choices that could have resulted from the three trials:

GGG	GDD
GGD	DGD
GDG	DDG
DGG	DDD

Each of these eight possible outcomes of three trials is equally likely to occur. But the boy chose the glove three straight times; this is the outcome GGG. If the choice were determined merely by chance, the event GGG had a 1/8 chance of occurring. Another way of saying it is to say that the probability of observing an outcome as likely as GGG is 1/8. If the experiment were repeated eight more times, another GGG situation could be expected to occur **by chance alone** at least once. The experimenter might be willing to conclude that a probability of 1/8 is good enough to say that he has proved the boy prefers baseball gloves to dolls, but most scientists would not make such a conclusion on that evidence. They need to be even more certain that they are correct in rejecting the null hypothesis and arguing for the alternative hypothesis that he really does prefer baseball gloves. In the social sciences, a probability level of 1/20 is usually considered to be the minimum level of acceptability, and many scientists would not be willing to make conclusions until they had seen results at a 1/100 level. In the case we have been using, we would have to run five trials and find the boy choosing the glove each of the five times to reach a probability level of 1/20; we would have to run seven trials with the boy choosing the glove all seven times to reach a level better than 1/100.

Even if the boy made his choice ten times in a row and each time chose the glove over the doll, one would not be able to say with complete certainty that the boy prefers baseball gloves to dolls because, even then, there is a probability of 1/1024 of having the ten-times-in-a-row choice occur by chance alone. For most of us and for most scientists, having the boy pick the glove ten times in a row by chance is such a rare event that we would conclude that the null hypothesis is wrong and that some alternative hypothesis must be selected. The probability pattern does not allow us to make a direct test of the hypothesis that the boy prefers baseball gloves to dolls. Instead, answers must be obtained from the indirect process we have just described.

Using the probabilistic pattern is an indirect manner for the public speaker to use in obtaining proof. The method never allows him to say that a particular conclusion is correct. It only allows him to say that the opposite of the conclusion has a high probability of being incorrect. The decision as to when an inference has been "proved" to be correct is an arbitrary one. For one person, three broken windows in a period of three months is enough evidence for him to decide that somebody is "out to get him." For another person, the same three broken panes of glass represent only a series of accidents, a rare event to be sure, but not a deliberate plot. Can a communicator ever be sure? No. He may become more and more positive, he may show more and more conclusively that his inference is likely to be the best one, but he can never be sure that what happened did not occur by chance rather than by design.

Another example will show how people may react to probabilities. This incident occurred when the author was just beginning college. I had been hired to sell soda pop during the Illinois State Fair and found myself working with a group of men who traveled from fair to fair all summer long. At night, after the day's work was done and the soda "butchers" had received their pay for the day, they retired to a small room under the stands to change clothes. Invariably, a card game or a dice game would be started, and after a long, hot day there was frequently a great deal of money in the game. One evening, when the money was piling up, an incident took place that indicated just how arbitrary our decisions are about probabilities. The man who owned the dice had just thrown his fifth 7 in a row and was about to throw for the sixth time. Just then, one of the bettors reached over and quietly laid an open razor on top of the pile of money. The shooter looked at the razor, looked at the dice, threw, and lost. He picked up what money he had not lost on the throw and left the room and the fair. Were the dice honest? I will never know. It is certainly possible to throw five 7s in a row, but the probability of that event occurring by chance is low. So low that the man with the razor decided he could no longer support the null hypothesis that said the dice were honest. He chose to support in dramatic fashion an alternative hypothesis— either the dice or the shooter were dishonest. He was operating on probabilities, although he may never have heard the term. The same problem faces any communicator who must accept and operate on inferences that must be established by using the probabilistic pattern.

The steps to use for assessing inferences by the probabilistic pattern include:

1. Determine what events are included in the situation. How many possible outcomes are there for these events? Determine on the basis of a chance estimate what the probability of occurrence of each event is. In the examples used, the probability for any one event was assumed to be equal to the probability for any other event. In some situations this is not the case, and each event in the situation will have a different probability.

2. Determine what the null hypothesis is. With three different events, each with an equal probability of occurrence, it may be hypothesized that the probability of event A is equal to the probability of event B is equal to the probability of event C ($\Pr A = \Pr B = \Pr C$). Remember the null hypothesis is based on the assumption that these events will occur by chance alone.

3. Determine what level of confidence is acceptable. If the results obtained could not occur by chance alone as much as 5 percent of the time, is this satisfactory? Or is a $1/10$ or a $1/100$ level better? The level is up to the communicator, but some level must be set up or no conclusions may be drawn.

4. Make the observations needed. These may be drawn from historical examples, be actual observations made about a group of people or ideas or events, or be observations made in the laboratory. Enough observations must be made to assure that the probability of occur-

rence can be computed so that the null hypothesis may be rejected if it is wrong. Observations should be collected at random so that any observation has as much chance of occurring as any other observation.

5. Determine how likely it is that the sequence of events observed could have happened by chance alone. This step should result in some fraction or decimal ranging from 0 to 1.00. One can never have a probability larger than 1.00 or smaller than 0.

6. Compare the figure obtained in step 5 with the level of confidence set in step 3. Suppose that the probability of chance occurrence of the sequence of events observed is 1/10. Suppose that the level of confidence desired was 1/20. The obtained probability is larger than the level of confidence. Therefore the null hypothesis may not be rejected, and the case has not been proved. On the other hand, suppose that the obtained probability figure was 1/30. This probability value is smaller than the level of confidence set up, and the null hypothesis may be rejected; one may then say the chances are that the inference is correct. The case will have been "proved" according to the standards set up.

This is the probability model. As described, it sounds completely different from the deductive model. But as we have already suggested, it really is related quite closely to the deductive model, and the relationship shows the limitations of the deductive model. Our discussion of the deductive model pointed out that it is difficult to establish the truth of the premises. But if the truth of the premises cannot be established with absolute confidence, no conclusion may be drawn about the truth of the conclusions, even if the syllogism is valid. Our discussion of the probabilistic pattern suggests that one might use this pattern to establish the truth of the premises one uses in a syllogism. Take the following syllogism, which is valid:

All animals suckle their young.
All men are animals.
All men suckle their young.

In this deductive argument, it has to be established that all animals suckle their young. It is, however, impossible physically to look at each and every animal in the world. So one must turn to induction and establish by use of the probability pattern that it is very probable that all animals suckle their young. However, any use of the probabilistic pattern may establish the truth of the statement only at some level of certainty that will be less than perfect. Because it cannot be established beyond the shadow of a doubt that all animals suckle their young, one may only say that it is highly probable that all animals suckle their young. Therefore, the conclusion that all men suckle their young may not be drawn with complete confidence.

The only deductive situations that may be established absolutely are those relatively rare situations in which **all** members of the class can be examined. For example, we could look at the statement, "Everyone in this classroom has blue eyes," and establish the absolute truth of the statement. But in those larger matters in which it is impossible for us to look at all cases, our look at the probabilistic pattern shows us one of the inherent limitations of the deductive pattern.

An inference based on the probabilistic pattern is a statement made about the world from a sample drawn from that world. Such an inference is no better than the results of the sample drawn. It is a generalization based on an examination of a portion of the events. Such generalizations play an important part in oral communication and in the decisions that lead an individual to become a communicator.

The functional pattern

The deductive pattern, the Toulmin model, and the probabilistic pattern were all developed in order to examine factual statements. Although they may be used by a speech communicator in speaking about policy questions, their main thrust has been in the area of questions of fact. The next two patterns we shall examine are more clearly related to an examination of policy questions.

In many areas of concern to the communicator, proof takes the form of indicating one or more functions that an event plays in determining the way an entire system operates. Called **functional explanations,** such proofs may also be termed **teleological** explanations, or proofs. Philosophers raise a number of objections to the use of functional explanations as proof, and their objections undoubtedly limit the kinds of situations and questions to which this pattern may apply. Nevertheless, functional explanations are accepted as proof by auditors and are used by communicators to make decisions. An understanding of functional explanations is thus important to the communicator.

During the late 1960s and early 1970s, many people in the United States have been concerned with the nature and quality of American life. What can we do about poverty? What will a dependence on computers do to the lives of people in the United States? Will air pollution prove to be a major factor in increasing disease? Will birth control help improve the quality of American life? These and similar questions form the core of current controversy. It is difficult to "prove" that the country will be damaged if computer use is not limited. It is difficult to show via the deductive route that poverty can be eliminated. Induction may help to provide some of the statistics on which the President and Congress will base new programs in pollution control, but it cannot establish firmly that one program is likely to be better than another.

In this situation, communicators have often used the functional pattern in order to establish the soundness of their positions. Those who are in favor of federal aid for schools attempt to explain their position by pointing to the role that schools play in our society and by indicating the importance of keeping a strong educational system. They then point out that some states either have not or cannot support schools of equal strength to those of other states, and they conclude by suggesting that in order to assure equal opportunity in education, the federal government has the right and the duty to aid the educational sector of our society. This is a functional pattern of proof, a pattern by which the speaker takes the function of an event or object or institution as a basis for making decisions. In the case we have cited, those opposed to federal aid for education also use a functional pattern to establish their position. They look at the role of the federal government and at the roles of the states and cities. They point out that in countries where education is controlled by the central government, the result has been either a totalitarian state or a weak educational system. Therefore they argue against federal aid to education. Again, a functional pattern is used to support a major conclusion.

Let us consider one of the arguments from the "Great Society" debates of the late 1960s as a further example of how the functional pattern may be used. President Johnson introduced the term "A War on Poverty" early in his administration. The debates in Congress resulted in a package of legislation and appropriation of money to carry out the program. The debates centered around a whole complex of smaller issues, and almost all of them were presented as arguments derived from a functional pattern. The proponents of President Johnson's program argued that the structure of our society was not such that the poor were an integral part of it. They argued that the role of the poor in our society was such as to drag down living conditions for the rest of society. They argued that if poverty could be eliminated, the entire society would reach heights never before attained.

The opponents argued that there has never been a society without its poor, that they are not created by others but rather they create themselves. They suggested that even if money were poured into the economy in an attempt to raise living standards for the poverty stricken, eventually this money would wind up in the hands of those who are not poor. In other words, they argued the way in which the society functions is such that the poor are an integral part of the structure, and that attempts made to change a part of the basic structure of the society would destroy it.

Without discussing the "rightness" of either position, let us consider the nature of the arguments used. On both sides, the arguments were functional—attempts to establish the desirability or reasons for a claim by showing how the claim is related to some larger structure. A scientist would use a functional explanation to understand the liver, showing what functions the liver plays in the operation of the body. A conservationist wishing to preserve a species from extinction would attempt to show the role the species plays in maintaining the balance of nature and the probable results to be expected if man eliminated the species. A college president attempting to convince a state legislature that his university should admit students from all parts of the United States uses a functional argument when he shows the legislature the role played by such students in broadening the education received by the majority of students in the university. A social scientist justifies his very existence, in part, by using functional analyses. He uses them to ascertain how social systems—e.g., the United States —perpetuate themselves by maintaining their structure and to demonstrate that changes in the social system are also likely to be accompanied by changes in the social structure.

How does one make a functional analysis? Three steps make up the process:

1. **Identify the total structure to be examined.** It might be the school system in a particular town or a city governmental structure. It could

be a structure as large as the "society of the United States" or as small as "the governing organization of my church." The total structure must be identified as carefully as possible, or the analysis will be made on elements that do not really play a part in it.

2. **Identify the elements of the total structure.** This is not always as easy as it may seem. Any structure may be analyzed on different levels, but the communicator is usually interested in a particular level of analysis for a given question. If the school system is the total structure, individual schools within the system might be used as the unit of analysis or classrooms within the system or grades in the entire system or principals, teachers, or even individual students. If the interest lies in raising individual teachers' pay, an analysis based on classrooms as the smaller unit might be inappropriate. In making the selection of the unit of analysis to be used in considering any total structure, the ultimate purpose of the analysis must be considered.

3. **Determine the role played by each of the units of analysis in the total structure.** This means more than merely indicating the immediate function played by some element within the total structure. It usually means that the analyst must also determine, if possible, what changes may be expected in the total structure if changes are made in any element within it. This means that the analyst must determine what **values** each element possesses and what changes in those values will mean to the structure as a whole. To use the school system again, take the teacher as the unit of analysis and ask what will happen to the school system as a whole if one group of teachers is treated differently from another group of teachers. If salaries for the science teachers are raised, what effect will this have on the other teachers? If new classroom facilities are provided for the high-school teachers in the system, what are the probable effects on the rest of the teachers in the system? This third step, therefore, is a crucial one, explaining not only the immediately observable function of the elements in any system, but also explaining how changes in those elements may be expected to affect the system as a whole.

Once an analysis has been made, the communicator will use the results to make decisions regarding his initial question. Decisions cannot be as precise with a functional analysis as with a deductive or probabilistic pattern. But when the communicator must make decisions affecting the structure of some social organization, and when an analysis of that structure in terms the function played by elements within the structure will assist in explaining the nature of the structure, a functional analysis is extremely useful.

Decision making is not always easy. To use the example of education, imagine that our analysis shows that we may improve the quality of education within the school system by raising teachers' salaries. We make that decision, but we are then faced with the necessity of raising the money to pay the additional salaries. At that time we are faced with the necessity of making another functional analysis in order to determine what the best way will be of raising the additional money. Can it be done by raising taxes? Can it be done by eliminating some teachers and having higher class sizes? Our initial decision has led us to make additional analyses and additional decisions that may then force us to change the original set of recommendations in order to accommodate the new data.

Once he has made a decision, the communicator will have the task of communicating it to an auditor or set of auditors. Here, the functional pattern is of extreme utility. Many audiences are not able to follow a deductive analysis of a situation. In fact, as will be discussed in Chapter 7, even well-educated groups are not able to follow deductive analyses very well. The same may be said for complicated probabilistic patterns of analysis. Statistics tend to become complicated, and an oral communication situation is perhaps the worst setting in which to attempt to present statistical information. The average listener has great difficulty in following or understanding such a presentation. Like the Toulmin pattern, functional analysis does not seem to have these limitations. In presenting materials to an audience, the communicator will find it very useful to structure his arguments, and perhaps even his entire speech, in the form of a functional analysis. The analysis may be simplified greatly while still retaining the shape and form of the functional pattern. The functional pattern is an analytic and communication tool that should be in the "toolbox" of every communicator.

The genetic pattern

Philosophers disagree on whether the genetic pattern of inference is a distinct type of inference or only a subclass of probabilistic patterns. The characteristics of the genetic pattern are distinctive, however, and it seems reasonable to present it as a distinctive type of inferential proof. Like the functional pattern, the genetic pattern is particularly applicable to the analysis of questions of public policy, rather than to factual questions.

The genetic pattern sets out the sequence of major events through which one system changes and matures into a present system. In this sense, therefore, the pattern could be called a **historical** pattern. It looks over the entire pattern of past events that seem to be connected with some present event and tries to suggest which of the past events contributes most to the present state of affairs. By abstracting the characteristics of the events thus isolated, the analyst attempts to predict the future direction that the system will take.

Assume that one wishes to ask what will happen if the Congress of the United States passes a bill severely limiting the availability of firearms to the American public. An opponent of such legislation might use the genetic pattern to attempt to defeat the bill. He would cite the instances of Germany, Japan, and other countries that severely limited the right of the people to own firearms before the Second World War and suggest that it was this restriction on citizens' liberty that led to the formation of totalitarian governments. Then he might turn to some of the Scandinavian countries that also limit firearm use and point out that it was this restriction that made it easy for the Germans to overrun these countries during the same war. In other words, he would pick out major events in history in an attempt to show that the best prediction one may make of the future is on the basis of the past. He would conclude that severely limiting the availability of firearms is not what the United States needs.

A proponent of such legislation, however, might also use a genetic approach to the analysis and presentation of his side of the question. He might point to the rising rate of crime in the United States and to the number of people shot with firearms purchased under uncontrolled conditions. A proponent of gun-control legislation might also single out the Second World War but use it to make a different point. He might show that much of the equipment left over from the Second World War has found its way legally into the hands of criminals. He would then suggest that such legislation does not destroy the rights of potential buyers but merely attempts to protect the rights of others.

The former example of the genetic pattern makes use of one of the most common subclassifications of the pattern, i.e., the argument from analogy or a parallel case. We attempt to show that the situation we are concerned with is similar to a situation in another place, and that consequences in our present situation will be similar to the consequences that resulted from the decisions made in the other place. A clear example of the argument from analogy is familiar to any college debater. This is the argument that the United States is much like Great Britain. A debater shows the points of similarity between the two systems and concludes that the two systems are essentially comparable. Then he goes on to show that Great Britain adopted some policy in the past, such as socialized medicine, and that the result of adopting such a policy has been to dramatically improve the health of the English people. He continues his argument to suggest that if the United States were to adopt socialized medicine, the country would obtain the same advantages for its people.

An example of the use of the genetic pattern more clearly tied to the historical development of a particular system might be found in the changes in trade restrictions for a country. Imagine that Congress is faced with a bill advocating high, protective tariffs for textiles. The proponents of the bill may carefully go back into history and attempt to show that the textile industry in the United States has been weakened every time tariffs were lowered to permit cheaper imports from other countries. They will suggest that weakening has meant people have lost their jobs and, even more important, the United States has suffered when a war occurred and we could not obtain imported textiles. The opponents of high tariffs also use the historical example to point out that high tariffs have traditionally meant higher prices to consumers in the United States and an increase in the inflation rate. Both proponents and opponents make use of the genetic pattern to trace how past actions have affected the textile industry itself, and how decisions made about this industry have affected the rest of the country.

The genetic pattern falls into three steps:

1. **Describe the system to be investigated.** The same cautions raised about the functional pattern may be raised about the genetic pattern. The system that is to be analyzed must be described precisely, and the level at which analysis is to take place must be described in detail.

2. **Describe the sequence of major events that led to the present situation.** This is obviously the most difficult step; it frequently leads to the kind of controversy we find today about control of firearms,

school education, or protective tariffs. Which events are the "major" ones? Which events should be ignored as unimportant in the development of an idea or a system? The analyst must have a set of assumptions upon which he bases his decision as to which events he chooses to analyze and which he chooses to ignore. They may be assumptions suggesting that economic events are more important than political events, that events involving leaders of a state or country are more important than events involving ordinary people, or that scientific developments are more likely to lead to changes in the system than developments in literature or film making. There is no way to determine absolutely which assumptions are better, but the communicator is forced to select on **some** basis the past events of the system he is interested in describing.

3. **Describe the causal chain that leads from the events selected to the present state of the system.** Again, this is not easy. As we have suggested before, causality can never be determined with complete accuracy. Look at such a simple event as a rainfall. What caused the rain to fall? Was it the presence of clouds bearing water, was it the passage of the cloud through a dust cloud, was it a drop in temperature causing the water to condense, or was it a lowered barometric pressure? For any given rainstorm, it might be one of these events or two or, most probably, a combination of all the possible causes. But the causality cannot be determined with perfect confidence. Even when a high correlation between two events can be shown, causality may be implied, but it can never be established with certainty. In spite of this impossibility of establishing causality with certainty, the genetic pattern demands that the analyst try to show the causal links between the events he has shown as important and the system he is describing.

These are the steps that set up a genetic pattern. Once the communicator has completed these steps, he may make decisions about his initial question. He might decide that firearms control would be unwise, that public education needs more governmental support, or that the police need more authority. His decision will be based on a genetic analysis.

The major objection to the genetic pattern has been implied, but it needs to be made explicit. It is unlikely that every event in the history of a social system will be selected for consideration as important to the present condition of that system. But when two people view the same system, the chances are very good that they will select different events as being important. The selection of different events may well lead to different conclusions regarding questions of public policy. Because all such selections of events are to some extent arbitrary, one cannot be positive he has selected the most meaningful events, or even that he has been able to find the most meaningful events amidst the jumble of events that seem to be related to the situation under discussion. This is a severe criticism of the use of materials from history, and suggests that the communicator might be well advised to look at other patterns of analysis before settling on the genetic pattern as his best choice.

In spite of the severe limitations of the genetic pattern, its persuasive qualities are very high. Many audiences will have great respect for the communicator who argues from history, who appeals to events in the past as illustrative of decisions to be made at the present time. For example, the decision of the United States to pursue the war in Vietnam was presented to Americans as an argument from history. It was argued that a careful consideration of previous instances of a nation faced with aggression yields the conviction that the best results are obtained when aggression is met firmly, rather than when loopholes are left for the aggressor nation. When we finally conclude the Vietnam conflict, it should serve future communicators as an argument that may be used against proposals to assist other countries in fighting their wars. Such arguments, made from a genetic pattern, have proved effective again and again and have proved effective quite apart from their actual probative value.

Summary

This chapter has discussed the problem of inference, a problem that arises when one must draw conclusions from various pieces of evidence or when one is confronted with an inference and must assess the quality of the inference. Five patterns were discussed in detail: the deductive pattern, the Toulmin pattern, the probabilistic pattern, the functional pattern, and the genetic pattern.

The deductive pattern, the Toulmin pattern, and the probabilistic pattern have their primary value in the analysis of questions of fact, although their use in assessing questions of policy was also shown. The functional pattern and the genetic pattern have their primary usefulness in attempting to assess questions of public policy; they were particularly recommended for their persuasive effect when used as organizing concepts for an actual presentation. The limitations of each pattern of analysis were discussed, and the strengths of each pattern were shown in terms of actual questions for which each might be used.

Motivational proof

In **Gulliver's Travels,** Jonathan Swift makes a religious controversy the basis for a war. Over the merits of opening eggs at the big end or at the little end, the little people of Lilliput embroil themselves in a bitter civil war. One can imagine orators from Lilliput rousing their people to patriotic heights by claiming, "It is immoral to open eggs from the little end," and "Only criminal conspirators would ever open an egg from the big end." The egg argument sounds silly, but it capsulizes the problem of the relation between judgmental statements and proof.

When proof is defined as the process of using evidence to secure belief, judgments seem to be ruled out as a source of proof. Judgments **do** form a kind of evidence, however, and their use in speech communication **does** lead to changes in belief. Judgments must be considered, along with observations and inferences, as a primary source of the materials that a speaker will use to secure belief in his ideas. There are several aspects to consider when we look at motivational proof. We must be concerned with judgments themselves and their nature and use in oral communication. We must be concerned with the relationship of the speaker himself to the proof situation, i.e., his own credibility in the communication situation. And finally, we must look carefully at patterns of analysis that are associated with motivational proof.

Judgments

In order to understand how the term **judgment** is used in this book, some understanding of the differences between observations and judgments is necessary. Listed below are four sentences that are clearly observations, or statements of fact, and four sentences that are clearly judgments:

Observations:

Gone with the Wind is one of the top ten money-making films of all time.
The Statue of Liberty was erected in 1876.
There is a positive relationship between smoking and lung cancer.
The Rembrandt painting "Aristotle Contemplating the Bust of Homer" recently sold for the highest price any painting had ever realized in an auction sale.

Judgments:

Gone with the Wind was the finest movie ever made.
The Statue of Liberty is the true symbol of the United States.
Smoking is a dirty, filthy habit.
The Rembrandt painting "Aristotle Contemplating the Bust of Homer" is undoubtedly the best example of the master's art.

Note the differences between the two sets of sentences. In the first four, some way in which to check the truth of the statement may be established. Old documents will give the date when the Statue of Liberty was erected. A list showing how much money was made by various films may be examined, disclosing whether **Gone with the Wind** was in the top ten. Any observation is capable of being verified in some fashion, even though it may be difficult or prohibitively expensive to do so.

The second four sentences, however, cannot be handled in the same fashion. There are no old records to indicate whether or not the Statue of Liberty is the true symbol of the United States. There is no way of ascertaining by a perusal of the records whether or not **Gone with the Wind,** or any movie, was the finest ever made. Not one of the second set of sentences can be verified. Checking with the physical world will never produce an answer regarding the truth of a judgmental statement. The only checking that may be done is with the maker of the statement. He may be asked if he believes that smoking is a dirty, filthy habit. Even if he says yes, his answer does not make it so for any one other person than himself. It merely indicates that someone believes that the statement is true.

The essential difference between an observation and a judgment lies in whether or not it can be verified. And the question of verification is dependent upon the relationship of the words used in the statement to physical reality. Observations stress the use of words that refer to physical reality, whereas judgments stress words that refer to personal or social reality. This distinction marks a difference in the kinds of meaning that are stressed in sentences of the two types and deserves further exploration.

Many words have their primary reference to an object or an activity that may be identified by anyone. These words carry a **denotative** meaning as their primary component. Such words as "sold," "smoking," "money," "husband," and "glass" are words that have as their primary meaning some agreed-upon relationship with an object or activity in the physical world. On the other hand, many other words do not have a primary relationship to the physical world. Their referent is some cognitive state within an individual. Words in this category have a primarily **connotative** meaning. Such words as "finest," "beauty," "dramatic," "prejudiced," and "disgusting" are words carrying a connotative meaning as their primary referent. There is no single place one may go to identify the meaning of words like these, except to the user of the word. "Disgusting" refers to an entirely different set of ideas and phenomena for a mother than for her three-year-old son. A beautiful woman for one man may not appeal to the man sitting next to him. These words are largely evaluative in nature and reflect man's eagerness to place values on the objects he encounters and the ideas he has.

But words cannot be divided into two piles, one of words carrying a denotative meaning and another of words carrying a connotative meaning. All words have both a denotative-meaning component and a connotative-meaning component. The word "Russian" carries with it a meaning of "citizens of the Soviet Union." This is a denotative meaning. But "Russian" to many people also represents a "bad" or "untrustworthy" individual. This is a connotative meaning. None of us would have much trouble in identifying a snake if we were to see one. We share a common denotative meaning for this word. But connotative meanings for the word range all the way from a feeling of favorableness for the reptile to feelings of abject horror and revulsion.

Even though all words carry both a connotative and a denotative component, usually one aspect rather than the other is emphasized. Thus, for most of us, the word "table" carries a largely denotative meaning. The word "beauty" carries primarily a connotative meaning. When words are used in statements, the statement may be classified according to the nature of the words within it. Thus a statement that uses words having primarily denotative meanings is likely to be an observation, while a statement that utilizes words carrying primarily connotative meanings is likely to be a judgment. Words that are fairly equally split between denotative and connotative meanings make statements difficult to classify as either observations or judgments. The best the communicator can do is to make some attempt to identify the intent of the person making the statement. Was he intending to make an evaluation or an observation?

Generally, in communication, words that carry largely denotative meanings do not give the communicator the same kinds of problems as words carrying largely connotative meanings. The reason for this difference lies in the way in which words are learned. Within any culture sharing the same language, the basic vocabulary is learned in about the same way by everyone. Every child learns to associate the word "dog" with the same class of objects. We have all learned, through the same process, approximately equivalent meanings for such words as "television," "toadstool," "fish," "education," and "mother." Thus people who speak English have a large group of words they may use with the expectation that equivalent denotative meanings will be recognized by their English-speaking auditors coming from the same culture.

Even on the denotative level, however, there are words that may take several different meanings, and there are objects for which several different words are used by different subgroups within the culture. For example, look at the word "school." One may use it to refer to the formal education system, to a specific place in a city, to a group of fish, to the process of learning, and perhaps to other kinds of activities. Only the context will reveal what the term is being used to denote in a specific situation. Similarly, the same object may be referred to by many different names. For example, "bream," "sunnies," "punkinseeds," and "gills" are among some of the names applied in different areas to the common sunfish. On the denotative level, the speech communicator must make sure that his auditors will have the same meanings as he does for the terms he uses in his statements. However, his task is relatively easy, because common meanings are held by large segments of the population.

On the connotative level, the problem is quite different, and this fact forms the basic question for this chapter. Connotative meanings are **not** the same for large segments of the population. Even when a group of auditors might tend to evaluate the same judgmental statement in the same way, the communicator cannot **know** that this is the case, and he has few ways of finding out that an audience has a common connotative meaning for a term. It is important to try to establish the kinds of connotative meanings held by individuals, for if a group holds common meanings for a set of terms, those terms may be used in judgmental statements, and they will be treated as observations.

It has already been emphasized that the judgment is a statement that emphasizes connotative meanings. Connotative meanings are personal to individuals and thus differ widely among individuals. However, connotative meanings, like denotative meanings, are learned through experiences with the world around us. The speech communicator may use a judgment as material to induce proof, because judgments depend for their formation on a prior series of observations.

Look at a simple judgment, and attempt to go through the steps that an individual might have gone through before he came to believe in it. Take the statement, "Harvard is the best university in the United States." What observations might lie behind an individual's willingness to believe in and make that statement? He might have observed some of the graduates of Harvard, noting that, over the years, they achieved positions or prominence in government and industry. He might have observed the number of graduates going on to graduate school. He might have noted the amount of money given to Harvard in endowments, the number of research grants made to the university, or the number of Nobel and Pulitzer prize winners teaching there. Or he could simply have read a series of statements, made by people he trusted, asserting that Harvard was the best university in the United States; trusting these sources, he is now willing to make the same judgment. Presumably, if one looked far enough, one could find a series of observations made by someone who arrived at a judgment after making the observations.

All judgments are made on some basis, and the speech communicator must locate the observations on which a judgment is based before he becomes completely willing to accept the judgment as proof. The problem is that some judgments are made on the basis of personal observation of a series of underlying events, and others are made after consideration of another series of judgments. To illustrate the latter situation, take the statement, "Sophia Loren is the world's most exciting woman." Such a statement is likely to be accepted as fact and used in proof situations by many individuals. What are the observations behind the belief? For many who would profess belief in the statement, the basis for the belief lies in having read in a newspaper or a movie magazine, that "Sophia Loren is the world's most exciting woman." Thus the only observation the individual would have made before coming to this particular belief is to have read the statement in some magazine or heard it from a friend. Somewhere, at some time, someone must have made a series of observations that led him to make the statement, but the speech communicator is likely to find it impossible to ferret out the original evidence on which the statement is based.

Statements such as "Harvard is the best university in the United States," and "Sophia Loren is the world's most exciting woman" are judgments that are held at a **peripheral** level in the belief system of most individuals. Beliefs held at peripheral level are likely to change drastically over a span of time and across subgroups in the culture. Look at the concept of beauty over the years. The teenager of today finds it impossible to understand why his grandparents considered Mary Pickford beautiful and almost as impossible to understand why his parents thought Rita Hayworth beautiful. Similarly, the teenagers' parents may find it impossible to understand why their sons think long hair is masculine or their daughters refuse to get a permanent. Standards in clothing change from year to year. Musical tastes change. Preferences in political oratory change. The late Senator Everett M. Dirksen of Illinois was pointed to as the last of the "great" orators, but the reason that his breed of orator is dying is that tastes in oratory have changed so that speakers with a style similar to Dirksen's are simply not elected.

Some beliefs are held more strongly and change only slowly over the years. In 1965 the first Medicare Bill was passed in the United States. Yet the idea was first suggested by President Harry S Truman in 1945, when it met with ridicule and general opposition. Furthermore, the idea had been debated in one form or another in the United States since the 1920s and in Europe since 1850. The values placed on government-sponsored medical care and the observations made about such a program changed only slowly over the years, but they did change. Individuals very seldom change their political-party affiliations over the years, but the nature of the propositions forming the party platforms does change. The Democratic Party has recently supported propositions that formed planks in the Socialist Party platform thirty years ago. The Republican Party today is not the Republican Party of Lincoln's time or even of Coolidge's. Judgments made about Medicare or about party platforms are also judgments made about authorities. Most individuals form their beliefs about medical care, about welfare programs, about taxation, or about government on the basis of the beliefs they hold about the individuals who make public presentations in these areas. Such beliefs, and the judgments made from them, form part of the **intermediate** level in an individual's belief structure. They may be held no more intensely than beliefs at a peripheral level, but they will be harder for the average auditor to change, and thus the communicator will have less success when dealing with judgments referring to the intermediate level.

Finally, judgments may be made in reference to very strongly held beliefs—beliefs about religion, about life, about mankind, and about an individual's self-concept. When an individual has made a judgment that "Lutheranism is the best religion," that "whites are better than blacks," or that "mankind is the highest form of life in the universe," he will tend to treat these judgments as factual statements. He will probably be very reluctant to change beliefs regarding such judgmental statements lying in the **central** level of his belief structure.

As stated previously, the speech communicator has two tasks. He must formulate and establish the statements or the ideas he believes in, and he must find ways of effectively communicating those ideas to others. From the discussion so far, a few suggestions seem appropriate:

1. The speech communicator ought to ascertain the basis on which he makes the judgments he intends to communicate to others. Sometimes, such an analysis will lead him to change the judgment or at least to search for more specific evidence to support the judgment.

2. The speech communicator ought to attempt to ascertain whether or not other individuals have made the same basic background observations he has. If not, he must supply the auditor with such data before he can hope to have the auditor arrive at the same judgments. This is particularly important in cases where the auditors may come from radically different backgrounds than the communicator.

3. The communicator must realize that a judgment in which the audience is likely to believe will have the same status as an observation. If one has made a series of observations and is willing to make the judgment that "**Gone with the Wind** was the finest movie ever made," he will treat that statement in exactly the same way as he treats the statement, "The Washington Monument is in Washington, D.C." Thus, when the communicator is fashioning an argument in order to induce belief in an idea, he may be able to use judgments and have them treated as observations.

4. The communicator must note that judgments are likely to be placed by the auditor into various levels of his own belief structure and to be accepted or rejected according to the centrality of the judgment being presented. A judgment that goes against a central belief is likely to lead the auditor to reject the entire argument. On the other hand, a judgment that is in line with the individual's central belief structure is likely to bring him to accept an idea even when there is little direct evidence to support it.

The speaker as a source of proof

For many observations, an individual can establish the truth of the observation by personal inspection of the evidence or events to which it corresponds. For some observations, and all judgments, this kind of personal inspection is impossible. The average American cannot go to Vietnam, Korea, or India to check the truth of statements made about those countries. Although the budget of the United States is published every year, it is so complex that only an expert can examine the document for evidence about levels of federal spending in various areas. Most communicators must rely on the observations of others and on a good reporting system to get those observations to them.

Judgments lie entirely in the minds of others, and we must depend on others to convey those judgments to us.

People who make judgments and people who make observations differ in their perceived ability as reporters or critics. One is inclined to trust the judgments of some and reject the judgments of others. When the same statement is made by two different communicators, and some auditors accept the statement from one communicator and reject it from the other, it may be said that either the **credibility** of the two sources is different or different characteristics in the listeners lead them to different decisions.

Source credibility is a phenomenon pointed to by Aristotle when he talked about the **ethos** of certain speakers. The phenomenon is more easily understood in terms of experiments showing differences in belief or attitude change caused solely by the credibility of the speaker. One such experiment was first made by Haiman,[1] and it has been repeated a number of times. Take a tape-recorded message that advocates socialized medicine. Then get a number of people and divide them randomly into two groups. Ascertain by means of an attitude test what attitudes are held toward socialized medicine by members of both groups. For group A, play the tape, and tell the members that the speech was made by a sophomore at Northwestern University. For group B, play the tape, and tell the audience that the speech was made by the Surgeon General of the United States. Then measure the attitudes of both groups again and determine how much attitude change there was in each group. The investigator should find, as did Haiman, that more members of group B than of group A changed to favor socialized medicine. Because the same tape was used for both groups, one must conclude that the difference in amount of attitude shift was the result of the influence of the source. The Surgeon General of the United States has more **source credibility** than a sophomore at Northwestern University.

The credibility we place on individuals is many times a judgment made about the individual. We say that "the President is a nice man" or that "John Wayne knows what he is doing." These are judgments—judgments made about the sources of the messages we listen to. For every individual, the sources from which he obtains information are arranged in a kind of hierarchy, with the most credible sources at the

[1] F. S. Haiman, "An Experimental Study of the Effects of Ethos in Public Speaking," **Speech Monographs,** 2 (1949), 190–202.

top and the least credible at the bottom. Thus, for one individual, the New York **Times** might be the most credible source and, for another, the minister of his church. For one individual, the president of the AFL-CIO might be a very credible source, while for another, the president of the United States Chamber of Commerce might serve as highly credible. Credibility also varies with the topic under consideration. The Secretary of State might be the most credible source when the topic is foreign policy, but the county agricultural agent might be more credible when the topic is hybrid seed corn.

Every source has a certain degree of credibility for an auditor, either positive or negative, and occupies a certain place within one's personal hierarchy of credible sources. But source credibility is not a unitary characteristic. Within the concept of source credibility at least three dimensions, or characteristics, may be distinguished, i.e., perceived by the auditor as possessed by the communicator. According to the communicator's degree of possession of these three characteristics, an auditor will tend to place more or less faith in his message. The three dimensions, as recently described by Berlo, Lemert, and Mertz,[2] are **trustworthiness, qualification,** and **dynamism.**

Trustworthiness comprises the general faith placed in an individual because of the position he holds or the record he has established over time for veracity. An individual perceived as trustworthy may speak on topics on which he is not an expert and be believed. For many individuals, their minister would place high in their belief hierarchy because they trust him, not because they feel him to be an expert on all subjects.

Qualification is specific competence in a particular topic and seems to be a less general trait than trustworthiness. An individual may be considered an expert on one topic and not on another. He will be believed when speaking on the first topic and not necessarily believed on the other. Dr. Linus Pauling, the Nobel prize winner, has high credibility when speaking about his major area of expertise in physics. He has much less credibility when speaking about foreign policy.

Dynamism is a different sort of characteristic from either of the other two. Some communicators are judged by auditors to be more dynamic

[2] David K. Berlo, James B. Lemert, and Robert J. Mertz, **Evaluations of the Message Source: A Basis for Predicting Communication Effects,** Research Monograph, Department of Communication, Michigan State University, 1965.

than other communicators. Dynamism is related to rate of speaking, amount of bodily action, tone of voice, and perhaps other character- istics that are difficult to describe. President John F. Kennedy, for example, was perceived to be a dynamic speaker, more dynamic than President Dwight D. Eisenhower, though he was not necessarily more credible. Dynamism is perhaps the least important of the three dimen- sions of credibility, although it may be the factor that proves most persuasive to an auditor. Given two people the auditor perceives to possess approximately the same degrees of trustworthiness and qualification, the individual judged to have the most dynamism will tend to have the higher credibility and thus more effect in an oral communication situation.

These three dimensions of credibility seem to be relatively indepen- dent of one another, although any speaker will possess varying degrees of all three characteristics. The independence of the dimensions is indicated in such statements as, "I don't think he knows much about the subject, but I don't think he would tell a lie," "I don't trust him very much, but I love to listen to him talk," or "It is too bad that he can't seem to get his ideas across, because he certainly knows what he is talking about." These are examples of situations in which an indi- vidual is perceived as credible in one dimension but not in another. It is also possible for an individual to be perceived as credible in all three dimensions of trustworthiness, qualification, and dynamism. In some of the studies that have been conducted, President Kennedy came across as an individual who was so perceived.

Source credibility is stressed when talking about judgments, not only because much source credibility is arrived at through judgments made about the source, but also because the auditor cannot check out judgments against reality. The best he can do is to check out the maker of the judgment and decide whether or not he will believe that the individual is credible. Thus the communicator may utilize source credibility in two ways. First, he may attempt to appear credible him- self so that the judgments he makes in his speaking will be believed. And second, he may use judgments that are quotations from individ- uals who are perceived as credible. Thus, in a speech advocating ex- tension of the Medicare Bill, the use of quotations from the President, from physicians, from hospital employees, and others interested in and appearing qualified to discuss the subject will bolster the argu- ment.

Some people have argued that credibility is "bad." They seem to believe that ideas should stand or fall on their own merit and that one should not take into consideration the personal characteristics of the individual presenting the ideas. As an ethical position, this argument may well have merit for the perfect world in which every auditor is a rational man. However, we do not live in such a world as yet, and auditors do respond to speakers and change their attitudes on the basis of the credibility they attach to them as the sources of messages. The effective speech communicator will realize this and attempt to make use of source credibility as an important factor that can lead to more effective communication.

Proof and motivational patterns

The title of this chapter is "Motivational Proof." Motivation becomes more important when judgments are concerned than when either observations or inferences are in question. The linkage between judgments and motivation is somewhat tenuous and depends on the way in which the term **motivation** is defined. Psychologists define it in various ways, and some feel that the term should be abandoned altogether because it has come to "mean all things to all people." Before deciding whether or not we should discard the term when discussing communication, however, let us look at some of the models of motivation that have been traditionally used and at the possible relationships between these models and judgments.

One model suggests that individuals continuously strive toward a more inclusive and stable organization of their own cognitive states. This model assumes that when an individual becomes the recipient of communication, he attends to the various messages and then tries to reconcile conflicting messages. The model assumes that man is rational, and it is only necessary to "give him the facts," and he will go to work in a completely sane, rational, logical fashion to "make sense" out of the world around him. It assumes that man has developed certain basic beliefs and assumptions. The auditor examines any messages he receives against the background of these beliefs and assumptions, and then either accepts or rejects any portion of a message in a manner consistent with his basic assumptions. The model further assumes that judgments are accepted **only** when they are seen as being consistent with previously held beliefs. Thus judgments play a part in decision making and attitude change only to the extent that they are seen as supporting observed sense data.

A second model of motivation, a reward–punishment paradigm, assumes that man does not distinguish among observations, inferences, and judgments but reacts solely to whether they are personally rewarding or threatening to him. With this model, the social system becomes extremely important in determining the ways in which man views information. When an individual listens to the expression of a judgment, he will tend to check reactions with others in his immediate social system and only then will he change or refuse to change attitudes, depending on the perceptions of the other members of his group. Group norms become an important determiner for the communicator in this model, because such norms indicate what will be seen as rewarding by the group and what will be seen as nonrewarding or even threatening. In such a reward–punishment model, man does not need to possess rationality but merely the ability to react to rewarding or nonrewarding situations in a consistent manner, i.e., the ability to learn. The communicator, operating under a reward–punishment model of motivation, would select judgments for presentation to an auditor on the basis of their rewarding nature to him, not necessarily because they fit logically into an argument.

A third model of motivation, a personality paradigm, suggests that man's central approach to attitude formation and change, and thus to the judgments he hears and makes, is one that emphasizes maintenance of the individual's self-image and self-integrity. He will accept messages that support his own personality structure and reject messages that disturb it. Rationality enters only accidentally into decision making if we support this model. Messages may actually be punishing to the individual's best interests, but if they support his personality, they will be accepted. The model assumes that individuals maintain their egos at different strength levels. An individual who has firmly established the structure of his own personality system tends to reject any information that would harm the system, whereas an individual who has left loopholes in his personality structure will be willing to consider messages that may seem threatening to him.

These three models of motivation overlap to some extent. Experimental evidence is still insufficient to establish one of the models as clearly superior to the others. Some of the evidence available, however, suggests that reception of judgmental information is partly dependent on an interaction between certain personality characteristics and the manner in which the materials are presented. For example, the model of man as a rational being suggests that materials cast in a rational form will be better received than materials appealing only to authorities as a reason for changing attitudes. In a study by Wagman,[3] people were divided into two groups depending on whether they were inclined toward an authoritarian personality or a nonauthoritarian personality. Then the groups were given messages that either appealed to "facts and reasons based on scientific study" or were based on "statements attributed to power figures." The results of the study showed:

1. The rational materials were more effective with nonauthoritarian subjects, whereas the statements from authorities were more effective with authoritarian subjects.

2. Some of the authoritarian subjects showed greater prejudice after the message than before. That is, they actually showed negative effects.

3. Some of the nonauthoritarian subjects reacted negatively to authoritarian messages designed to make them less liberal. They actually became more liberal than before.

This study illustrates some of the problems that the communicator faces in attempting to make use of judgments in his messages. Available evidence tends to show that the ways in which man behaves depend on a number of different factors, and a single model of motivation is insufficient to account for all the differential effects that might be produced by using judgments in messages.

The models of motivation just presented may help the communicator in organizing his own thinking about the relationship between the judgments he uses in his speeches and the reception of those speeches by auditors. Even if none of the three models may be considered to explain motivation entirely, some combination of the three will provide an adequate model for the communicator. Each of the three models assumes that certain characteristics that an individual possesses or develops through learning either facilitate or hinder the persuasive power of any message. It is possible to integrate relevant portions of the three models of motivation by examining the relationship between general persuasibility and certain personal and social

[3] M. Wagman, "Attitude Change and Authoritarian Personality," **Journal of Psychology**, 40 (1955), 3–24.

variables found in auditors. Such an examination shows that individual traits are related to general persuasibility. That is, if an individual possesses trait X and research shows trait X is positively related to persuasibility, the communicator should find it easier to get acceptance of his message from the individual possessing trait X than from an individual who does not possess trait X. A number of such relationships have been studied. It is, of course, impossible to assert that the relationship exists just because a single study says it does, but the relationships reported below, both positive and negative, represent the best conclusions possible at this time.

1. There seems to be a positive relationship between persuasibility and low self-esteem. The individual who possesses feelings of anxiety or feelings of inadequacy seems to be somewhat more persuasible than the one who does not have such low self-esteem.[4]

2. There is some support for the proposition that individuals who are overly aggressive or hostile in their interpersonal relations are less persuasible than those who are not so aggressive or hostile.[5] Furthermore, additional information tends to show that with teenagers and even younger children, hostility and low persuasibility are positively related with boys but that the relationship does not hold for girls.[6]

3. There is some support for the hypothesis that individuals who reveal an authoritarian personality pattern are more persuasible than those tending toward nonauthoritarian patterns.[7] This finding, however, has to be considered against those of the Wagman study, reported above, which does not disagree with this general finding but suggests that there may be an interaction between the type of message presented and authoritarianness.[8]

4. A number of studies have investigated the relationship between general persuasibility and intelligence. In general, they tend to show that when subjects are drawn from equivalent educational levels, no significant relationships are found between persuasibility and in-

[4] Irving L. Janis and Peter B. Field, "Sex Differences and Personality Factors Related to Persuasibility," in **Personality and Persuasibility**, eds. Carl I. Hovland and Irving Janis (New Haven: Yale University Press, 1959), pp. 55–68.
[5] **Ibid.**
[6] **Ibid.**
[7] Harriett and Elaine Graham, "Personality Correlates of Persuasibility," in **Personality and Persuasibility**, pp. 69–101.
[8] Wagman, "Attitude Change and Authoritarian Personality."

telligence.[9] It should be noted, however, that these results do not extend to amount of education as a variable. Although intelligence is positively related to level of education, most studies tend to separate the two variables. When this is done, there seems to be a negative relationship between amount of education and persuasibility.

5. There is much research evidence to show that females are generally more persuasible than males. In most of the studies, the differences between men and women in terms of persuasibility are very small, but they are statistically significant and show in a number of studies.[10] Whether this finding is a real sex difference or whether it occurs because of educational differences, because of the nature of the message being presented, or because of some personality trait that is more prevalent in women than in men, has not yet been determined.

Studies of this type should provide at least some aid to the communicator in his task of predicting how auditors will respond to the material he presents. Certainly, present research has not been able to provide all the information one would like to have about audiences. Future research should help with this problem of predicting. For the time being, however, the communicator must be able to utilize information drawn from the motivation models already described and, combining it with what persuasibility research is able to provide, make estimates about the ways in which auditors will react.

The next, and last, chapter will be concerned with some of the ways in which messages may be presented to obtain belief from a listener or set of listeners. However, judgment seems more closely tied to motivation than to any of the patterns of proof previously presented. Therefore, it seems reasonable to consider some of the patterns of organization and some of the problems arising when judgments must be used to secure belief in a proposition.

We have already indicated that judgments cannot be "proved" because their truth lies within an individual and not in physical reality. Thus, in a formal sense, we can never establish the truth of a judgment through use of the deductive pattern, the Toulmin pattern, or the probabilistic pattern. However, one **can** frequently secure belief in a judgment through use of one of these patterns of arranging and presenting materials. Assume that a speaker wishes to secure

[9] **Personality and Persuasibility,** pp. 237–238.
[10] **Ibid.,** pp. 238–240.

belief in the statement, "Harvard is the finest university in the United States." He might make use of an inductive pattern by organizing a number of statements to which the auditor would agree; having obtained agreement to those statements, the communicator would enhance the probability that the listener will accept his main conclusion. For example, he might use the following argument:

> Harvard has the highest-paid faculty in the United States.
> More faculty members hold Ph.D.s at Harvard than at any other institution.
> Harvard students have the highest average entrance-test scores.
> Harvard has the largest endowment of any institution in the United States.
> Harvard has had more Nobel and Pulitzer prize winners on its staff than any other institution.
> Therefore, Harvard is the finest university in the United States.

This is **not** formally correct. But **if** the communicator has presented enough statements, **if** the listener agrees to the truth of those statements, and **if** the listener agrees that those statements are related to the conclusion, then the listener ought to be more inclined to agree with the conclusion than if the conclusion had been presented in isolation.

Any of the other patterns of proof presented in Chapter 5 may be adapted in order to strengthen the possibility that a judgment will be accepted by an audience. The communicator must remember, however, that those patterns were developed to be used with factual and policy propositions, not with judgments.

Judgments emphasize values, and a judgment is a statement that places a value on some object, event, or contemplated activity. Values range along a continuum, however, and the speech communicator may choose the intensity of value he places on the object or event with which he is concerned. The intensity level chosen may well be related to the acceptance level the audience has for the judgment. Below are three judgments that vary in the level of acceptance they might have for an audience:

> 1. The proposal to require people on relief to give up their television sets is the most reprehensible suggestion ever to come from the City Council.
> 2. The proposal to require people on relief to give up their television sets represents poor judgment on the part of the City Council.

3. The proposal to require people on relief to give up their television sets needs further clarification and elaboration on the part of the City Council.

These three judgments range from intense to slight in the degree of believability asked of any auditor. Is it possible to say that the more intense the degree of belief asked of the auditor, the more persuasive the message will be?

Little experimental evidence is available in this area, but some evidence would suggest that the answer lies with the relationship between the auditor's original belief and the intensity of the judgment being presented. An individual who was already negative toward the City Council and already felt that most of its activities were poorly carried out would respond favorably to judgment 1. It fits with the expectations that he already has about the City Council. However, an individual who is favorably inclined toward the City Council and who tends to believe that its activities are usually well carried out is probably not going to accept the extreme statement represented by judgment 1. He might have no difficulty in accepting judgment 3 but would refuse to accept judgment 1 on the grounds that "this is what the opposition always says." On the other hand, a strong opponent of the City Council will certainly be willing to agree with judgment 3 if he is willing to agree with judgment 1. Thus the chances are that judgment 3, the least extreme of the three statements, will have more chance of being accepted by all factions. This suggests that the speech communicator is always better off using judgments that represent less intense attitudinal positions when he wishes to gain acceptance from the largest portion of an audience.

Some research suggests that auditors may not know a logical argument when they hear one but that they do like the appearance of logicality in the arguments presented to them.[11] If this is true, then it is probably also true that the same individuals will appreciate a "reasonable approach" in the presentation of judgments. This is the best conclusion that can be made about the intensity of appeal used in a specific case.

This conclusion, however, needs to be modified for one type of situation. There are times when a communicator will not care whether or not he obtains agreement from all members of the audi-

[11] Erwin P. Bettinghaus and James P. Swinney, unpublished research.

ence; he is more interested in a subgroup of the audience. For example, in the Congressional election campaign of 1970, Vice President Spiro T. Agnew deliberately attempted to divide his audiences rather than to unify them. By making reference to the opposition in terms a Democratic audience could not possibly accept, such as calling several Democratic candidates "radical-liberals," Agnew tried to win more acceptance from members of the Republican Party. In essence, his speeches attempted to draw the difference between the two parties more sharply than they might ordinarily be perceived. In such a situation, our conclusion that the less intense judgment is usually the more effective statement does not necessarily hold.

A second situation, also exemplified by party politics, in which the less intense statement is not necessarily the most effective, is seen in the political convention. In our national political conventions, the television medium broadcasts speech after speech, all loaded with extreme statements about the wonders of one party and the treacheries of the opposition party. A communicator may well wonder about the advisability of the "reasonable approach" when viewing such a convention. However, here the audience is already committed to support of the party, and the party leaders are merely attempting to intensify belief in the candidates selected and the platform presented. In making extreme statements, the party leaders run little risk. They know that they could not attract members of the opposition party even if they were to use the reasonable approach; and they are more interested in raising the emotions of the party faithful to the heights required by a tough campaign than they are in attracting support from neutrals. Such use of the intense statement, however, does not necessarily imply the successful use of such judgments in changing audience attitudes. Rather, the situation is such that the audience already has beliefs consistent with the position taken in the intense judgment, and the judgment merely serves to reinforce or intensify the previous belief position of the auditor.

Conclusions about the use of intense or extreme judgments in proof situations have to be made on the basis of an analysis of the type of situation encountered. Given an audience with strong beliefs, an extreme judgment may be used to reinforce or strengthen those beliefs. Given an audience the speaker wishes to divide in some way, extreme judgments may serve to strengthen that subgroup which the speaker wishes to reach while alienating the remainder of the audience. Given a situation in which the speech communicator wishes to secure belief from the maximum number of individuals, a less intense judgment is the most effective.

Fear appeals present another problem in motivational proof. Suppose that a communicator wants to reduce accidents on American highways. He certainly may present statistical information or other types of observations and inferences to show that certain safety measures will help to reduce accidents. But he may also attack his problem by presenting a series of judgments. Such judgments may attempt to scare the listener into doing something about his own driving record or into supporting stiffer licensing procedures. He might say, "Bad drivers are dangerous to your health." Are such attempts to use judgments effective in producing belief?

A number of studies have been completed in this area. An early study by Janis and Feshbach examined the effect of strong, minimal, and intermediate fear appeals in messages designed to get high-school students to brush their teeth. The strong fear-appeal messages pointed to the number of cavities that would occur and drew eloquent word pictures of the results of not brushing. The intermediate and minimal fear-appeal messages became progressively more "rational" in their presentation. The results showed that what Janis and Feshbach called the minimal fear-appeal message was the most effective form of the communication "in that it elicited (a) more resistance to subsequent counterpropaganda and (b) a higher incidence of verbal adherence, and perhaps a greater degree of behavioral conformity to a set of recommended practices."[12] They found that the intense appeal was the most effective form in arousing interest and in raising emotional tension, but was not the form that seemed to result in ultimate changes in attitude.

A more recent study by Hewgill and Miller[13] casts some doubt on the generality of the findings in the Janis and Feshbach study. This study showed that the nature of the threats made in the message was the most important element in deciding the effectiveness of the message. Hewgill and Miller were concerned with civil defense. Messages were constructed appealing to listeners to take certain civil-defense mea-

[12] Irving L. Janis and Seymour Feshbach, "Effects of Fear-Arousing Communications," **Journal of Abnormal and Social Psychology,** 48 (1953), 78–92.
[13] Murray A. Hewgill and Gerald R. Miller, "Source Credibility and Response to Fear-Arousing Communications," **Speech Monographs,** 32 (1965), 95–101.

sures. Some forms of the message made strong fear appeals, suggesting that failure to take the measures could result in disaster for the individual or the country. Others suggested that disaster would result for the individual's family. The findings showed that minimal fear appeals were better than strong appeals except when an appeal was made with respect to the auditor's family. A strong fear appeal in which the health or safety of the listener's family was threatened proved to be the most effective.

Obviously, more research is needed on this topic. A conclusion from the studies to date might be that fear appeals are effective when the object of the appeals is highly valued. When the appeal is made toward individuals or objects that are not so highly valued, more rational appeals will be more effective.

We should note that we have discussed the subject of fear appeals in connection with the presentation of judgments. However, fear appeals may be attached to observations and inferences as well as to judgments. Such appeals seem to have most of the characteristics of judgments and may be successfully used in the presentation of arguments.

An appeal to fear is only one of the types of appeals that may be used by the communicator. Appeals may be made to other types of human drives, such as hunger, thirst, patriotism, and gregariousness. These areas have not been carefully studied, and suggestions for presentation cannot be made. The communicator should recognize that appeals to other motives are certainly possible and should be considered when making decisions about the most effective way of presenting materials to an audience.

Summary

Judgments are statements that place values on the objects and events of the world around us. To the extent that they are believed, they are treated and acted upon in exactly the same fashion as observations and inferences. Belief in a judgment depends on the credibility of the communicator presenting the judgment, the characteristics of the auditor who listens to the judgment, the pattern of presentation of the judgment, and the nature of the appeal used in presenting the judgment.

SEVEN

Strategy and tactics in message preparation

When the communicator has collected and evaluated evidential materials on any topic, he must then make decisions about the position he will take regarding a conclusion. Our previous chapters on evidence and modes of proof are designed to help the communicator arrive at such decisions. After he has made his own decisions, he then faces the necessity of communicating them to others. At this point in the communication process, a great many questions are likely to present themselves. Should the audience be given all the information that the speaker used to make his own decisions? What if it has been a complicated question and there are restrictions on the amount of time the communicator will have with his audience? Is there some best pattern that may be used to present his materials? Will the nature of the audience help dictate the way in which speech materials are to be presented? Some of these questions have been considered in other volumes in this series. Selection of materials, use of language, audience analysis, and general arrangement of evidence are taken up specifically in other volumes. This chapter is concerned with some problems related to the arrangement of materials for proof situations, communication situations in which the intent of the speaker is to induce or change auditor belief in a proposition or series of propositions.

The differences between various kinds of proof materials have already been discussed, and suggestions have been made regarding the use of proof materials in evaluating conclusions. In Chapter 5, we suggested that five approaches may be used in evaluating evidence leading to the support or rejection of factual or inferential statements. These five approaches, the deductive pattern, the Toulmin pattern, the probabilistic pattern, the functional pattern, and the genetic pattern, are used by the communicator in making his decisions. However, they are not necessarily the best methods of later communicating those decisions to an audience. For example, audiences would have real difficulty in following the presentation of a series of classical syllogisms, no matter how useful such a pattern might have proved in the communicator's initial analysis. The average listener has difficulty whenever he is expected to listen to complicated arguments. Even when materials are presented in written form, as in an editorial, great difficulty is experienced in deciding whether or not the conclusions actually follow from the evidence introduced. Yet written messages **can** be read and reread until the reader figures out if the argument is to be believed. Under most circumstances, the auditor **cannot** relisten to a speech. Either he is convinced the first time, or he rejects the argument. What the speech communicator needs is a method of organizing the materials he finds in such a manner as to make it likely that an auditor will follow the argument easily.

The Toulmin pattern, earlier introduced as a pattern for the analysis of factual questions, may be modified to provide such a method of organizing speech materials. Although it was originally designed to be used in the analysis of factual propositions, it may be easily adapted to policy propositions and used with any of the proof patterns we have looked at in this volume. Stephen Toulmin's basic ideas have been expanded for the formal debate situation by Douglas Ehninger and Wayne Brockriede in their book **Decision by Debate**[1] and by Russel R. Windes and Arthur Hastings in **Argumentation and Advocacy.**[2] This chapter, however, presents the Toulmin organizational pattern as adapted for communication situations in which the speaker wishes to induce belief in some proposed **policy.**

[1] Douglas Ehninger and Wayne Brockriede, **Decision by Debate** (New York: Dodd, Mead, 1963).
[2] Russel R. Windes and Arthur Hastings, **Argumentation and Advocacy** (New York: Random House, 1965).

Figure 3 shows the Toulmin pattern in its simplest form. It makes use of only three of the six elements of the pattern—the evidence,

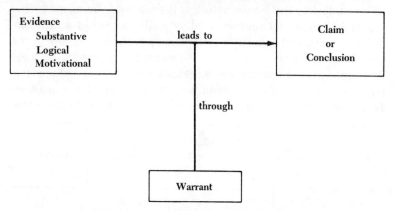

Figure 3. Simple Toulmin Model

the claim, and the warrant. Such an argumentative arrangement may be useful in many situations. Below are three arguments that make use of only these three elements in arriving at a claim:

a. Inflation is increasing rapidly in the United States (**evidence**). Individuals on fixed incomes are being hurt by the increase in inflation (**evidence**). The poor and the black and the young are being hurt by inflation (**evidence**). We must move to a policy of strict wage and price controls in order to control inflation (**claim**). We must take this step in order to protect the health of millions of people in the United States (**warrant**).

b. The United States has been fighting in Vietnam for over ten years (**evidence**). The United States has been trying to negotiate with the North Vietnamese in Paris for over two years without success (**evidence**). We should immediately withdraw all our troops from Vietnam (**claim**). We must take this step because it is obvious that we can win neither a military victory nor a negotiated settlement (**warrant**).

c. Many high-school students do not have the opportunity to go on to college because their parents do not have enough money to send them (**evidence**). The federal government ought to make scholarships available to all such students (**claim**). The nation cannot afford to have its human resources wasted because parents do not have enough money (**warrant**).

Each of these three arguments could be expanded by adding more evidence to support the claim made. Adding such evidence, however, does not destroy the simple nature of the argument being made. But the reader might well question whether audiences would accept conclusions presented in such a simplistic fashion. Adding any of the other three elements—support for the warrant, reservations, or qualifiers—may help to improve the believability of the claim being made. Figure 4 shows the basic pattern with the addition of the qualifier. This more complicated arrangement is shown in the example below:

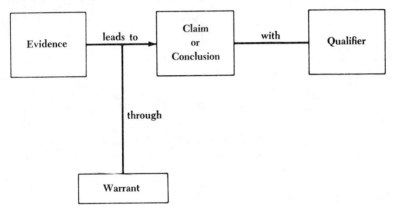

Figure 4. Simple Toulmin Model with Qualifier

The United States has been fighting in Vietnam for over ten years (**evidence**). The United States has been trying to negotiate with the North Vietnamese in Paris for over two years (**evidence**). It is likely that (**qualifier**) we should immediately withdraw all our troops from Vietnam (**claim**). We must take this step because it is obvious that we can win neither a military victory nor a negotiated settlement (**warrant**).

In a similar fashion, the speaker may consider adding the other elements within the pattern until very complicated arguments are reached. The example below makes use of all six elements of the Toulmin pattern as they were shown in Figure 2 in Chapter 5 (p. 80):

More than half of the world's population goes to bed hungry at night (**evidence**).

The world has more than doubled its population in the last thirty years (**evidence**).

Present figures show that the world will again double its population to approximately six billion by the year 2000 (**evidence**).

With present agricultural methods, the world cannot sustain even a minimum health standard with six billion people, says Dr. X of the World Health Organization (**evidence**).

We must institute a program of world population control within the next few years (**claim**).

Such a program should probably (**qualifier**) be administered by the United Nations (**claim**), since only the United Nations may be said to truly represent the entire world (**warrant**).

Unless nations move within the next few years to institute their own population-control programs (**reservation**) or unless a general world war begins (**reservation**), the United Nations, which Secretary Dag Hammarskjold once said was the one remaining hope of civilization (**support for warrant**), must seek cooperation of the world in making life on this globe possible for mankind (**restatement of claim**).

This is a complex argument, yet all the propositions within it may be analyzed by use of the Toulmin pattern. Furthermore, although the argument has been stripped of many of its rhetorical qualities in order to save space, it would, with a little polish, be a perfectly acceptable and appropriate argument to use in an actual speech. The arrangement of its parts is much as we would expect to find in an actual speech communication situation.

The Toulmin pattern, when viewed as a method of arranging speech materials, shows great flexibility. The "pieces" of the Toulmin pattern may be used to arrange any of the other proof patterns we discussed in Chapter 5. Figure 5 shows the deductive pattern arranged in terms of elements of the Toulmin pattern. Remember that, in general, the deductive pattern is one in which a specific conclusion is derived from more general propositions, as when we conclude that Socrates is mortal from consideration of the propositions that all men are mortal and that Socrates is a man. To present this conclusion to an audience in exactly this form, however, may not be very persuasive. The Toulmin pattern allows us to retain the valid conclusion we have arrived at, yet present the material to an auditor in a manner which may have more believability for him. In doing so, the communicator will find it useful to include the use of a warrant—as in Figure 5— that indicates the relationship between the evidence and the claim. This use of a warrant is necessary because the form of the argument,

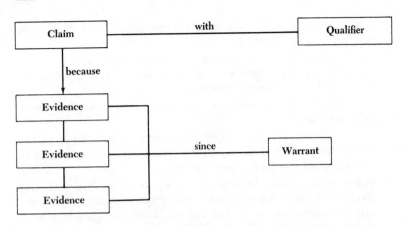

Figure 5. Toulmin Elements in Deductive Form

which is present in using the deductive pattern as a tool of analysis, is obscured when using an arrangement that makes it easy to listen to the argument but does not show its logical form. An example of a deductive argument arranged according to the Toulmin pattern might be:

> The United States is probably (**qualifier**) not justified in continuing to fight in Vietnam (**claim**).
>
> After all, few nations have won a war after fighting for over ten years (**evidence**).
>
> And most nations enter wars for economic reasons, but the United States has no economic interests in Vietnam (**evidence**).
>
> And most military disputes are best settled at the bargaining table (**evidence**).
>
> Because these reasons are logically related to the Vietnamese war (**warrant**), we should get out of Vietnam (**restatement of claim**).

Note that this argument does not pretend to show the auditor the exact way in which the speech communicator originally analyzed the argument and arrived at his conclusion. It merely uses the Toulmin pattern as a convenient way of organizing the materials that the communicator has gathered so as to make the conclusion or claim that he has reached believable to the auditor.

Figure 6 shows an arrangement of the Toulmin elements into a pattern that may be used in arranging materials drawn from a probabilis-

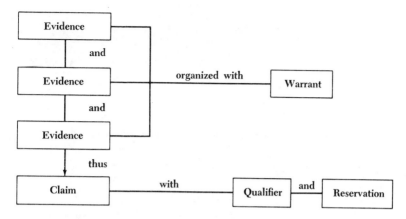

Figure 6. Toulmin Elements with Probabilistic Form

tic pattern of analysis. The probabilistic pattern is characterized by use of specific pieces of evidence. Again, the figure shows the use of a warrant, qualifier, and reservation to explain what might have been evident to the communicator in arriving at his original conclusion. An example of the use of the Toulmin elements in arranging materials from a probabilistic pattern might be:

There was serious inflation during the Civil War in the United States **(evidence)**.

There was serious inflation during the First World War in the United States **(evidence)**.

There was serious inflation during the Second World War in the United States **(evidence)**.

Since these were all major wars in our nation's history **(warrant)**, it is very likely **(qualifier)** that our current inflation is due to our involvement in the Vietnamese war **(claim)**, if we can agree that the Vietnamese war is a major war **(reservation)**.

This pattern resembles the probabilistic pattern very closely. However, rather than presenting all the statistics that the communicator gathered in order to arrive at his conclusion, the presentation to the audience stresses the major pieces of evidence alone and specifically includes the use of a warrant, which might be merely implied in the original analysis stage.

The functional pattern is more specifically concerned with the

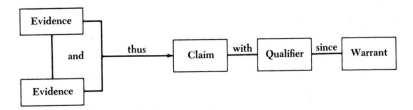

Figure 7. Toulmin Elements with Functional Form

analysis of policy questions than is either the deductive or probabilistic pattern. Figure 7 shows the Toulmin pattern adapted to the presentation of functional arguments. Remember that the essential nature of the functional argument is that it looks at the various parts of a process, such as the educational system, and attempts to derive a conclusion from an analysis of the way in which the process is functioning. Evidence drawn from the analysis of one structure is compared with evidence drawn from another structure, and the claim or conclusion attempts to show that there is a relationship between the various pieces of evidence. In the functional pattern, the warrant serves to connect the two structures by showing that they are similar in nature and may thus be compared. An example of a functional argument cast into the terms of the Toulmin pattern might be:

> Every major culture and society throughout the world's history has had a large percentage of poor people as an integral part of that society (**evidence**).
>
> In those few societies that have tried to eliminate poverty, the end result has been to make a few people even richer, while the poor seemed to grow even poorer (**evidence**).
>
> It is probable (**qualifier**) that the United States should not attempt to eliminate poverty (**claim**), since we do not wish to produce a culture with really sharp divisions between rich and poor (**warrant**).

Obviously, this functional argument could be complicated in many ways. We could introduce more evidence. We could use a warrant to show that the structures are actually related to one another. We could introduce a reservation suggesting that our claim was true only if the present structure was actually related to those we introduced as evidence. But the example will serve to illustrate the use of the Toulmin elements in arranging a functional argument.

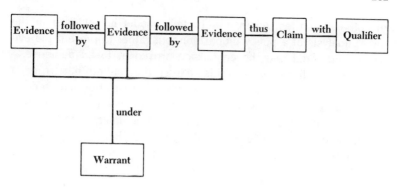

Figure 8. Toulmin Elements with Genetic Form

The genetic argument is also one designed for the analysis of policy statements rather than questions of fact. Figure 8 shows the use of the Toulmin elements arranged in a typical manner for the presentation of a genetic argument. Although a genetic argument need not involve history, the most typical genetic arguments involve arguments from historical facts. The following argument shows the use of Toulmin elements in a typical genetic argument:

> Germany severely limited the right of its people to own firearms before the Second World War, and this helped lead to a totalitarian state (**evidence**).
>
> Japan severely limited the right of its people to own firearms before the Second World War, and this helped lead to a totalitarian state (**evidence**).
>
> Norway limited firearms ownership before the Second World War, and this weakened the country so that it was an easy prey for the German armies (**evidence**).
>
> Since the best way we have of predicting the future is by looking at the past (**warrant**), then probably (**qualifier**) the best policy for the United States to follow is to refuse to limit firearm ownership in any way (**claim**).

Note that in this argument the warrant serves to show the way in which the three separate pieces of evidence are related to one another and to the claim that follows. The argument could be further elaborated by use of some support for the warrant or by use of a reservation that would note that the United States is similar in important respects to the other countries. Again, the Toulmin model is not used in the initial analysis of a policy proposition, but rather to present the evidence uncovered and the conclusion arrived at to an audience.

As we have discussed it in this chapter, the Toulmin pattern is an aid to the communicator in organizing his materials prior to presenting them to an audience. The pattern does **not**, however, give the communicator any rules to follow in evaluating an argument that has been constructed according to any of the patterns already suggested. In part, as we have suggested in previous chapters, no set of rules exists allowing a communicator to make decisions in policy areas with the kind of precision that he might desire. Two steps, however, are possible. First, the elements of the Toulmin model may be examined and suggestions made regarding the possible effect that **mistakes** such as omissions or errors in constructing any of the patterns might have on an auditor. Second, awareness of some of the common mistakes that people make in reasoning, i.e., **fallacies,** may improve the chances of the communicator in avoiding such mistakes in the arrangement of his materials.

Mistakes in proof patterns

A mistake in proof, for the purposes of this discussion, comprises any error in argument construction likely to lead an auditor to refuse to believe the conclusion **because of the error.** The nature of belief patterns in auditors, not formal validity, is the primary consideration. Such mistakes may be made with any of the six elements used in the Toulmin pattern.

The most frequent mistake in introducing **evidence** is the failure to use enough evidence for the claim made. Seldom is a broad claim supportable by a single piece of evidence or a single quotation. It is too easy to find counterevidence in most policy areas, and unless the communicator has presented enough evidence to overcome the possible weight of any counterevidence, he is not likely to be believed. Even when the communicator himself is convinced that one or two pieces of evidence are sufficient to establish some conclusion, it may be that an auditor will demand more evidence. It is extremely difficult to answer the question, "How much evidence is enough?" Perhaps the best rule to follow is to suggest that the communicator examine the evidence he has collected and attempt to determine whether it is

(1) convincing to himself and (2) at least sufficient to counter any of the pieces of opposing evidence that may exist.

A second mistake frequently made in the presentation of evidence is a failure to use evidence that is related to the claim made. For example, the United States recently cut off the program by which Mexican migrant labor was imported every year to aid in harvesting American crops. In 1965, cherry growers in Michigan refused to harvest much of the crop, letting it rot on the trees. It could be argued that the failure to allow Mexican pickers into the United States resulted in the cherry crops being allowed to rot. The growers took their action, however, because of the low price offered for their cherries, and the low price was the result of bumper crops in previous years. To argue that the evidence regarding the policy on migrant labor was the cause of cherries rotting on the trees would be a failure to use evidence actually related to the claim made.

The most frequent mistake made in using the **warrant** is to base a claim on a warrant that is insufficient to justify the claim in the eyes of the audience. For example, a communicator may believe that any statement by the President of the United States is sufficient to justify the claim being made. An audience is not likely to take such a view and would reject the claim if the warrant is of such a nature. In genetic arguments, the most frequent warrant is that the present may be best judged in terms of the past. Today, however, many young people would deny that what previous generations have done should be a determiner of what the present generation should do. The use of such a warrant in genetic arguments might well lead to rejection of the claim by young audience members.

A second error in using the warrant is in the reference to superstition as the basis for a claim. To claim that some policy will now be necessary because an individual failed to throw salt over his left shoulder, or because a mirror was broken, is obviously to use a warrant that cannot relate evidence to claim.

These examples are easy to see, but more subtle examples may be cited. To support a claim "because God says so" or to support a claim "because the stars are right today" is to make the same mistake in use of the warrant.

Faulty **claims,** as has already been mentioned, frequently result when more is claimed than the evidence can justify. President Kennedy would not have been justified in arguing from a single eyewitness report smuggled out of Cuba that a threat to the United States actually existed. He might have been justified in concluding from such an eyewitness account that the country should attempt to obtain aerial photos of the supposed missile sites. In the first case, the evidence is related to the claim, but there was not enough evidence. In the second, the evidence is also related to the claim, but the claim is more believable.

Mistakes in **qualifiers** are difficult to detect. They generally result from using a qualifying word or phrase so strong that it cannot be accepted by an auditor. To say that the population explosion is an important world problem is to use a qualifier few might object to. To suggest that the population explosion is "the most" important world problem is to use a qualifier that might be hard for many people to accept.

Too often, the error made with the **reservation** is to ignore it. Yet few claims may be made without considering other possible changes in policy or other potential moves that might alter the claim made. Another mistake is to make too many reservations, so many that the applicability of the claim to anything in the real world is hard to see. This is the result of an overabundance of "ifs." The speaker may say, "If this happens, and if that happens, and if this should come to pass, then X will be likely to happen." He may be reaching an accurate conclusion, but because of the many limitations he has placed on the claim, it is likely he will not receive the attention his claim deserves.

The same mistakes made in using evidence may be made with the **support for the warrant.** The communicator may fail to use sufficient support to justify the warrant made, or he may use supporting materials that are not related to the warrant. Either error may result in rejection of the warrant and thus in audience disbelief concerning the relationship between evidence and claim.

Any of the reasons cited in this brief analysis might result in rejection of a claim by an auditor. It must also be pointed out, however, that rejection may occur even if the argument is well constructed. Belief depends far more on the predispositions of the auditor than it does on the manner in which an argument is constructed. However, the manner in which the communicator constructs his messages may result in acceptance by an individual who has not already determined his own position or who has not previously considered the matter.

Fallacies

A fallacy may be defined as a mistake in reasoning—a mistake that leads an individual to consider evidence and to draw a claim from it that is not justified. The study of fallacies is very old, dating back as far as Aristotle. Some of the mistakes noted in the last section may be classified as fallacies, but there are other common fallacies that will be discussed here. A communicator is warned against fallacies for two major reasons. First, fallacies are formal mistakes in reasoning that may occur with any of the five proof patterns we have discussed. Thus they may lead the communicator himself to make decisions that are not actually justified. Second, many of the more common fallacies are recognizable by auditors and will result in the rejection of any claim advanced by the speech communicator.

The classical fallacy is the one sometimes labeled **post hoc, ergo propter hoc** ("after this, therefore because of that"). This is the error of assuming that merely because one event follows another in time, the earlier event caused the later to occur. In its ridiculous form, one might argue that because I broke a mirror yesterday, I fell and sprained my ankle today. The assumption in most superstitions, old wives' tales, and magic is a **post hoc** assumption. It argues that because one thing happened, another must be tied to it. But merely following in time is not **sufficient** grounds to argue cause, although it is a **necessary** ground. Both the genetic pattern and the functional pattern are particularly susceptible to allowing a **post hoc** argument to creep into the analysis framework.

Faulty causal reasoning probably accounts for more mistakes in proof situations than any other single fallacy. It is important to establish cause in many policy areas, and it sometimes seems irresistibly plausible to argue that the appearance of one new phenomenon is the cause of another. After the Second World War, for example, many people argued that rainstorms, floods, and indeed any natural disaster must be caused by the dropping of atomic bombs. Indeed, many people still believe that weather is influenced by atomic testing, in spite of the complete lack of scientific support of such a theory. But it seems so believable that it has received support even from educated individuals. Timing alone, however, may never be used to account for causality.

One of the most common arguments in favor of the Medicare Bill, passed in the United States in 1965, was that a similar program works in England and therefore should work in the United States. This represents the use of a single piece of evidence, with a claim that it will also apply to the United States. This example illustrates **faulty analogy.** The warrant is unstated, but it must be a belief that the United States and England may be compared with respect to medical care. The argument is a functional one, with use of the special case called an argument from analogy, i.e., reasoning from what happened in one situation to what will happen in another situation. Let us suppose that two people are both members of the same church—they share the quality of similar church membership. Reasoning from analogy would argue that because the people share church membership and because one individual is, for example, a poor credit risk, the other must also be a poor credit risk.

At some point, every analogy must break down, because there will always be some place where two objects or two events differ in nature or degree. However, if there are many points of similarity between two events, it is possible to generalize from the results of one event to the probable result of another. Faulty analogy results when two events, structures, or people are not alike in the characteristics that are being compared or in characteristics relevant to those being compared.

A special case of faulty analogy is sometimes called the **fallacy of composition.** It is the assumption that what is true of individuals alone will be true of individuals in a group situation. It is the warrant that says the whole is equal to the sum of its parts. This may be true, but it is likely that people will behave differently in groups than they behave separately. A recent example of the fallacy of composition is to be found in the argument that because price supports help the cotton farmer, the wheat farmer, and the soybean farmer, therefore price supports for all commodities would help all farmers. Maybe this is the case, but the analogy between cotton, wheat, and soybeans does not necessarily hold true for beef, pork, and chicken.

A **dilemma** results when two or more claims seem equally justified from the evidence presented. Some dilemmas are real. An individual who is asked to choose between having an operation that could result in death on the operating table and not having the operation and running the risk of dying of cancer may face a real dilemma. A **faulty dilemma** results when one of the claims is specious—when the evidence really does not justify making the claim. A faulty dilemma may also result when there is a third possible alternative that has not been stated. For example, take the case of a farmer who is raising wheat for sale. It could be argued that such a farmer can never get ahead: when he produces an excellent crop, the price falls, and when the price goes up, his crop will probably be poor. Either way, the argument goes, the farmer never wins. This is a faulty dilemma, because it fails to consider the possibilities of government price supports as aids to the farmer. It is also faulty in that it makes the assumption that when one farmer has a poor crop, all other farmers will also have poor crops.

Any dilemma may be examined in two ways. Either one may question whether all possible claims have been exhausted, or one may question whether all the claims suggested have the same merit. The speech communicator, using one of these two methods, may frequently make sense out of what appears to be a hopeless situation.

Psychological fallacies are those in which a decision is made and presented to an audience on the basis of the emotions stirred up by the language used in constructing the argument, rather than the evidence or the proof pattern used. The use of **emotional language** in argument construction may assist in obtaining belief. But it may, equally, prevent belief changes and is likely to do so when an auditor has been relatively neutral or mildly opposed to the claim being advanced. Emotive language capable of such effects may occur in phrases such as, "There are always a few malcontents to oppose real progress," "The Governor is always ready to support legislation that will lead to increased freedom," "This action denotes a deliberate plot against the company," "This piece of legislation is the most pernicious that could have been offered," and "The speaker harangued the audience."

It is certainly proper and sometimes desirable to use words to arouse vivid imagery, but such use may obscure the specific action that is being advocated. The communicator must be sure that the audience he is addressing will be inclined to agree with him, or he runs the risk of having his argument rejected for irrelevant reasons.

Special pleading is the fallacy of presenting only materials that tend to support the claim one wishes to present when other evidence is clearly present. For example, the Surgeon General of the United States released a report that tended to show a relationship between smoking and lung cancer. Other research organizations came forward to argue that their research had not shown the kind of relationships shown in the Surgeon General's report. However, their research had been supported by some of the large tobacco industries. It is frequently the case that scientists will disagree, particularly on a complicated subject, but the arguments from the research organizations supported by the tobacco companies became suspect. They seemed to be a case of special pleading. In other situations, special pleading occurs when individuals argue differently from the same set of materials. A "good buy" for me is a "steal" for you. What is "aggression" for one country becomes "preventive war" for another. These are, again, cases of special pleading.

When a communicator has a position that cannot be adequately supported, he may attempt to draw attention away from it by directing attention to some side issue. This is considered **drawing a red herring,** or false trail, over the real issue. In court, a lawyer with a weak case may attempt to show that his client attends church regularly and gives money freely to charity. This tends to obscure the fact that the individual may have obtained the money he donated by embezzlement.

Another way of introducing a red-herring argument is to throw out so much evidence in a speech that the really relevant evidence is obscured. The communicator is giving all the evidence, but he introduces evidence that is not material to the decision and embeds the important materials in a sea of trivia. The auditor finds it impossible to separate the relevant from the irrelevant.

There are other fallacies that could be considered in this section, but most of them have been discussed in other sections within the book. Some of the logical fallacies have been covered in the discussion of proof patterns in Chapter 5, while other psychological fallacies have been discussed in Chapter 6. It should be pointed out that fallacious arrangements of materials make it difficult for the communicator to arrive at a considered decision regarding some area of policy concern. Such arrangements may also make it difficult to reach a set of auditors with an effective message. Although many of the fallacies we have discussed seem extremely persuasive arrangements of materials and might well result in changes in audience belief, there are serious pitfalls for the communicator when he allows fallacies to creep into his speech arrangements. For those trained to detect fallacies, the argument may carry little weight. If a fallacy is present and is rejected by an auditor, the communicator may find that this rejection carries over to a rejection of the remainder of the materials. For those wishing to see clearly the relationships between evidence and claim, the fallacy is disturbing and unconvincing.

Placement of materials

This section will consider two problems in speech tactics: Where does the communicator place the most important materials within the message? What differences result from listening to messages the communicator has garbled in some way? We are not concerned with the effects of argument importance or garbled messages on the amount of learning that occurs, except as learning is related to changes in belief. In neither of these two areas of concern has sufficient research been completed to make possible any final recommendations, but the research available is provocative and deserves consideration.

Let us assume that I have examined some evidence and have arrived at a general policy decision that I would like to communicate to others. The chances are that some of the materials I have will be more important than others, in terms of relating them to the claims I am making and in terms of the impact I expect them to have on an auditor. Where do I place the important information within my speech? Should I place it first, where it will hit the auditor immediately? Should it go in the center of the speech, after I have been able to interest the auditor in the speech? Or should it be the last thing I tell him, so that it will remain fresh in his mind?

There are a number of studies and reports concerning the effect of order.[3] The most general conclusion that may safely be drawn from these studies is that placing the most important issue either first or last is preferable to placing it in the middle. No study shows a preference for a pyramidal arrangement. The studies seem fairly well split between those tending to show a preference for placement first, and those tending to show a preference for placement last. None of the findings shows marked preference for either first or last position. However, a study by McGuire[4] suggests that placing materials seeming to appeal to the needs of the audience first, then following

[3] See specifically Carl I. Hovland et al., **The Order of Presentation in Persuasion** (New Haven: Yale University Press, 1957).
[4] **Ibid.**, p. 136.

them with somewhat less desirable materials, will produce more effect. Studies by Cohen[5] tend to support the McGuire findings.

Many other factors are more important than the order in which materials are placed. The commitment of the auditor to the topic being discussed, the number and nature of speeches that precede his speech, and the nature of the subject matter discussed undoubtedly all play a part in the way materials will be received. In the situation where these other considerations have been taken into account, and when the task of the communicator is first to obtain the attention of the auditor to the subject and then to interest him in the materials, perhaps the best conclusion is that the strongest materials should be placed first within the speech.

The other problem for this section is much clearer. Imagine that as a speaker I am relatively careless in my use of grammar. I mix up my words at times and make grammatical errors. What effect will this have on the perceptions of my audience? There are two studies in this area, one dealing with the effects of grammatical error on comprehension and opinion change and one dealing with the effects of switching statements out of normal order.

The first study is by Sencer,[6] who looked at the effects of grammatical error. He produced a series of messages and varied the number of grammatical errors within them. The same materials were in each message, but some messages had many more than the normal number of tense errors, gender errors, misspellings, and the like. The results are interesting. They show that the readers of the messages had little trouble in understanding the content of the message, but they resented having to read messages with a great number of grammatical errors. There was significantly less opinion change when the messages had a great number of grammatical errors than when they had few errors, even though the content of the messages was the same in all cases, and even though the readers understood both sets of messages.

The second study was by Darnell,[7] who produced a message with fifteen statements arranged in a deductive pattern, with a claim at the beginning and supporting materials neatly arranged below the

[5] **Ibid.,** pp. 135–136.
[6] Robert A. Sencer, "An Investigation of the Effects of Incorrect Grammar on Attitude and Comprehension in Written English Messages," unpublished doctoral dissertation, Michigan State University, 1966.
[7] Donald Darnell, "The Relation Between Sentence Order and the Comprehension of Written English," **Speech Monographs,** 30 (1963), 97–100.

claim. Then he systematically varied the order of presentation by switching statements around in the messages until he had seven messages, ranging from one in perfect order to one with a maximum amount of garbling. Again, there were few significant differences in comprehension. But there were highly significant differences in opinion change in favor of the messages in relatively logical order versus those that were garbled.

Apparently, what is operating in both these cases is a set of expectations about messages on the part of auditors. The listener expects messages to be free from error, and when they are not, he resents it and takes out this resentment by refusing to believe what is being claimed, even though he may arrive at perfect understanding of the message. Results similar to the two studies mentioned above were discovered in a study regarding delivery. Good delivery was preferred to poor and resulted in more opinion change, even though, in both cases, the speaker was the same and the message was the same.[8]

This **violation of expectations** probably governs much of the way in which auditors approach the oral communication situation. The speech communicator may use evidence carefully. He may make his own decisions about a conclusion to be drawn on the basis of a careful look at the evidence as it is placed within one of the proof patterns we have discussed. But if, in presenting those materials to an audience, he violates the expectations we all have of the ways in which speeches ought to be constructed and delivered, he will fail to have the effect he wants. If proof is the process of using evidence to secure belief in a proposition, it is equally a process of using evidence in ways that will not violate the expectations of an audience. Poor arrangement, poor language use, poor structure, poor style, and poor delivery may lead a communicator to fail to "prove" a case to an audience although the case may well have been proved to his own satisfaction.

Summary

This chapter has discussed the presentation of materials relating to a communicator's policy decisions. The Toulmin pattern was used as

---

[8] Erwin P. Bettinghaus, "The Operation of Congruity in an Oral Communication Situation," unpublished portions of doctoral dissertation, University of Illinois, 1959.

a device for organizing materials prior to presentation to an auditor. We have shown that the six elements of the Toulmin pattern—evidence, claim, warrant, support for the warrant, qualifier, and reservation—may be used as an organizing device for materials previously analyzed under the deductive, probabilistic, functional, and genetic patterns of proof. Complex arguments as well as relatively simple arguments may be handled with the Toulmin pattern.

The chapter also considered mistakes arising from the use of the Toulmin elements and looked carefully at a number of fallacies in reasoning. Such fallacies ought to be avoided, since they may make it impossible for the communicator to arrive at conclusions adequately representing his evidence. The use of fallacies, although possibly persuasive to some audience members, will not be persuasive to many others, and should be avoided. Finally, the chapter discussed how important the placement of materials and message-design errors are to successful change in audience beliefs.

Selected bibliography

Bem, Daryl J. **Beliefs, Attitudes, and Human Affairs.** Belmont, Calif.: Brooks/Cole Publishing Co., 1970.

Berelson, Bernard, and Steiner, Gary A. **Human Behavior: An Inventory of Scientific Findings.** New York: Holt, Rinehart and Winston, 1960.

Berlo, David K. **The Process of Communication.** New York: Holt, Rinehart and Winston, 1960.

Bettinghaus, Erwin P. **Persuasive Communication.** New York: Holt, Rinehart and Winston, 1968.

Braithwaite, Richard Bevan. **Scientific Explanation.** New York: Harper and Brothers, 1960.

Brown, Roger William. **Words and Things.** Glencoe, Ill.: The Free Press, 1958.

Cherry, Colin. **On Human Communication: A Review, a Survey, and a Criticism.** Cambridge, Mass., and New York: The Technology Press of Massachusetts Institute of Technology and John Wiley and Sons, 1957.

Cohen, Arthur R. **Attitude Change and Social Influence.** New York: Basic Books, 1964.

Dewey, John. **Logic: The Theory of Inquiry.** New York: Henry Holt, 1938.

Direnzo, Gordon J. **Concepts, Theory, and Explanation in the Behavioral Sciences.** New York: Random House, 1966.

143

Ehninger, Douglas, and Brockriede, Wayne. **Decision by Debate.** New York: Dodd, Mead, 1963.

Fearnside, W. Ward, and Holther, William B. **Fallacy: The Counterfeit of Argument.** Englewood Cliffs, N.J.: Prentice-Hall, 1959.

Festinger, Leon. **A Theory of Cognitive Dissonance.** Stanford: Stanford University Press, 1957.

————. **Conflict, Decision and Dissonance.** Stanford: Stanford University Press, 1964.

Friedman, Norman, and McLaughlin, Charles A. **Logic, Rhetoric and Style.** Boston: Little, Brown and Co., 1963.

Hall, Edward Twitchell. **The Silent Language.** Garden City, N.Y.: Doubleday, 1959.

Hovland, Carl I., and Janis, Irving L., eds. **Personality and Persuasibility.** New Haven: Yale University Press, 1959.

————, Janis, Irving L., and Kelley, Harold H. **Communication and Persuasion: Psychological Studies of Opinion Change.** New Haven: Yale University Press, 1953.

————, et al. **The Order of Presentation in Persuasion.** New Haven: Yale University Press, 1957.

Kemble, Edwin C. **Physical Science, Its Structure and Development.** Cambridge: The M.I.T. Press, 1966.

Lippmann, Walter. **Public Opinion.** New York: Macmillan, 1922.

Miller, Gerald R., and Nilson, Thomas R. **Perspectives on Argumentation.** Chicago: Scott, Foresman and Co., 1966.

Newman, James R. **What Is Science?** New York: Simon and Schuster, 1955.

Newman, Robert P., and Newman, Dale R. **Evidence.** Boston: Houghton Mifflin Co., 1969.

Ogden, C. K., and Richards, I. A. **The Meaning of Meaning.** New York: Harcourt, Brace and Co., 1945.

Rogers, Everett M. **Diffusion of Innovations.** New York: The Free Press, 1962.

Rokeach, Milton. **The Open and Closed Mind: Investigations into the Nature of Belief Systems and Personality Systems.** New York: Basic Books, 1960.

————. **Beliefs, Attitudes and Values: A Theory of Organization and Change.** San Francisco: Jossey-Bass, Inc., 1968.

Rosenberg, Milton J., et al. **Attitude Organization and Change.** New Haven: Yale University Press, 1960.

Rosnow, Ralph L., and Robinson, Edward J. **Experiments in Persuasion.** New York: Academic Press, 1967.

Scheibe, Karl E. **Beliefs and Values.** New York: Holt, Rinehart and Winston, 1970.

Schramm, Wilbur Lang, ed. **The Process and Effects of Mass Communication.** Urbana: The University of Illinois Press, 1954.

Smith, Alfred G. **Communication and Culture.** New York: Holt, Rinehart and Winston, 1966.

Taylor, James Gordon. **The Behavioral Basis of Perception.** New Haven: Yale University Press, 1962.

Tolman, Edward Chance. **Behavior and Psychological Man.** Berkeley: University of California Press, 1958.

Toulmin, Stephen. **The Uses of Argument.** Cambridge, England: Cambridge University Press, 1958.

Whitehead, Alfred North. **Modes of Thought.** New York: Macmillan, 1938.

Index